Fabulous Turned-Wood Projects

John Hiebert, Harm Hazeu,
Tim Bergen, & Henry Bergen

Sterling Publishing Co., Inc. New York
A Sterling/Tamos Book

A Sterling/Tamos Book
Sterling Publishing Co., Inc.
387 Park Avenue South
New York, NY 10016-8810

Tamos Books Inc.
300 Wales Avenue
Winnipeg, MB Canada R2M 2S9

© 2005 John Hiebert, Harm Hazeu,
Tim Bergen, Henry Bergen

Distributed in Canada by Sterling Publishing
c/o Canadian Manda Group, 165 Dufferin Street
Toronto, Ontario, Canada M6K 3H6
Distributed in the United Kingdom by GMC Distribution Services,
Castle Place, 166 High Street, Lewes, East Sussex, England BN7 1XU
Distributed in Australia by Capricorn Link (Australia) Pty. Ltd.
P.O. Box 704, Windsor, NSW 2756, Australia

Design S. Fraser and A. Crawford
Photography Jerry Grajewski, Grajewski Fotograph Inc.
Tim Bergen and John Hiebert

National Library of Canada Cataloging in Publication Data

     Fabulous turned wood projects / John William Hiebert ... [et al.].
Includes index.
ISBN 1-895569-88-5
     1. Turning. I. Hiebert, John, William 1920-
TT201.F32 2004   684'.083   C2004-905737-5

Library of Congress Cataloging-in-Publication Data

Fabulous turned-wood projects / John Hiebert...[et al.].
     p.cm.
"A Sterling/Tamos book."
Includes index.
ISBN 1-895569-88-5
1. Turning. I. Hiebert, John.

TT203.F33 2004
684'.083--dc22   2004017596

10 9 8 7 6 5 4 3 2

Tamos Books Inc. acknowledges the financial support of the Government
of Canada through the Book Publishing Development Program (BPIDP)
for our publishing activities.

Note If you prefer to work in metric measurements, to convert inches to
millimeters multiply by 25.4

ISBN-13: 978-1-895569-88-9
ISBN-10: 1-895569-88-5

For information about custom editions, special sales, premium and
corporate purchases, please contact Sterling Special Sales
Department at 800-805-5489 or specialsales@sterlingpub.com.

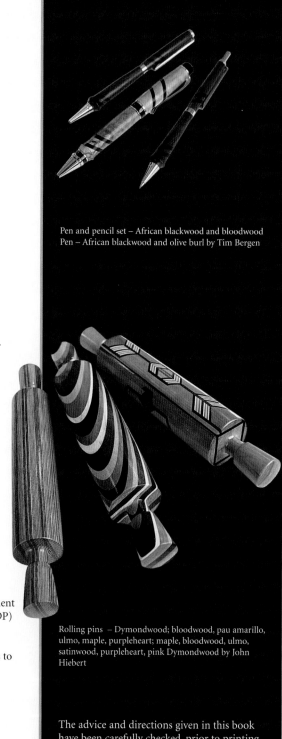

Pen and pencil set – African blackwood and bloodwood
Pen – African blackwood and olive burl by Tim Bergen

Rolling pins – Dymondwood; bloodwood, pau amarillo,
ulmo, maple, purpleheart; maple, bloodwood, ulmo,
satinwood, purpleheart, pink Dymondwood by John
Hiebert

Contents

Preparatory

Introduction	4
Getting Started	6
Safety	6
Woods to Consider	8
Wood Seasoning	10
Tools	11
Measuring	12
Tool Sharpening	12
Basic Procedure	12
Finishing	15

Woodturning Projects

Henry Bergen	16
turning vases	17
balancing logs	19
turning bowls	20
wood cuts	20
candleholders	22
John Hiebert	24
pink rolling pin	25
striped rolling pin	25
thunderbird	
rolling pin & cutting board	27
thunderbird bowl	32
wine cooler stand	34
winged chess bowl	38
lighthouse salt & pepper mills	41
Harm Hazeu	44
gavel & stand	45
scroll work plate	47
patterned vase	49
decorated walnut bowl	53
keepsake box & lid	56
applewood candlestick	59
Tim Bergen	61
pen and pencil sets	62
oak and cherry bowl	66
oak and cherry goblet	70
segmented walnut bowl	73
maple leaf bowl	84
candlesticks	91
kaleidoscope plate	93
Index	96

Woodturning Artists

Henry Bergen does plain lathe turning and works with blocks of unprocessed wood selected for grain, color, and knots or burls for decorative interest.

John Hiebert enjoys novelty woodturning combining plain lathe work with ornamental techniques and laminated pattern design.

Harm Hazeu is a master woodworker and does decorative woodturning that ranges from cut out scroll work to laminated patterns.

Tim Bergen creates intricate patterns for decorative art woodturning. The wood pieces are arranged and laminated to produce colorful exotic patterns.

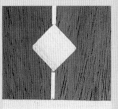

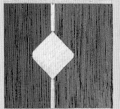

Introduction

The lathe is one of the oldest and most important machine tools. It introduced wood turning and this art has been practiced for at least 3500 years. In fact, ancient Egyptian tombs contained turned artifacts and the techniques used then were essentially pulling a cord wrapped around a work (supported between two fixed centers) back and forth to rotate the work so a sharp cutter could be applied to shape the work. The geometrical symmetry of turned wood had great appeal and this popular crafting quickly spread to other countries. Gradually this sit-on-the-ground method of turning evolved to a standing position and by 1700 pole and tree lathes were in use throughout Europe. In fact, the word *lathe* derives from *lath* or pole. Before this Leonardo da Vinci had experimented with lathe forms, progressing beyond the pole lathe to the flywheel lathe, but his work was not taken seriously. Later, by 1771 in France, turners recognized the great energy storage of the flywheel and this basic lathe form was generally adopted, although it was modified and improved over the years.

The work produced on the plain lathe was and still is simple in design. Its beauty depends on the choice of wood, the grain pattern, and the form created. Most objects created on a plain lathe (headstock, tailstock, and cutting tool) were practical and attempts to make them decorative were accomplished by wood color and texture as well as carving or a cut out design. This plain turning was practiced for many centuries. More elaborate ornamental turning required improved lathe equipment such as the slide rest and cams or templates mounted on the lathe. These were used to fine advantage to make *rosework* or patterns that looked like rose petals. Also when the spindle moved back and forth along the lathe axis, wavy lines were produced on the work and this was called *swashwork*. These patterns allowed for more elaborate designs and increased decorative artistry. By the 19th Century ornamental wood turning was very well established, especially in England which took the lead in developing lathe technology. As patterns became more intricate computer technology was used to develop and lay out designs and draw plans in much the same way an architect plans a building. The resulting specialized art is providing a whole new dimension for woodturning.

4

Turned crab apple vase: interesting grain pattern – Henry Bergen

Over the years woodturners have become more proficient and as the lathe's possibilities advanced utilitarian bowls and vessels became more decorative not only in shape and design but also in wood choice and wood combinations. Many pieces were made only for the creative beauty they displayed. To further enhance this decorative art woodturners began to create patterns within the work. Many different woods were laminated in such a way to make a design within the turned structure. Now the work had not only beautiful form and graceful lines but also a specific pattern arranged within the work created by different layers of wood colors and grains.

Today there is a tremendous resurgence of interest in woodworking and its special area of turning. Hobbyists seek to expand their work to bring turned wood beyond the practical to a form that defines their own vision. These master woodturners are developing new techniques and graceful designs that are admired everywhere. Yet technical masterpieces rely on the beauty of natural wood for complete artistry. A well turned and polished wood bowl or a beautifully shaped vase are by themselves art objects. Such pure wood forms combining natural richness and elegance of design create woodturning art.

The turned wood pieces in this book represent the work of four men who approach woodturning as a way of expressing the form they envision when they look at the grain and color of a wood piece. Each woodturner has developed techniques and use of tools that allow special effects, and all of these are carefully explained in the following pages. You will find simple lathe work that depends for effect on wood choice and turning skill as well as wonderful wood creations decorated with patterns and cut out design.

Combining and layering wood to make patterns is especially effective and these techniques are also given. The project pieces range from relatively easy to more complex, but the steps to make them are outlined and patterns and color photographs show how each step is achieved. Choose any of these designs and add your own creative ideas to make your own decorative turned wood art.

Segmented walnut bowl: red oak and walnut – Tim Bergen

5

◇ Getting Started

The lathe is the basic tool of the woodturner's craft and care must be taken to choose the one suited to your needs. In fact by using only a lathe and a few cutting tools you can create wood objects that are both practical and beautiful. Basically lathe work is spindle or faceplate turning. Spindle turning or centerwork is used for rolling pins, table legs, spindles, etc. while bowls, vases, and other open top objects involve faceplate turning. For spindle turning a spur at the head and a live center at the tail are used to hold the object to be turned. For faceplate turning a 6 in x 6 in x ½ in thick piece of scrap wood is screwed to the faceplate. When a bowl blank is fastened to this, turning can begin to shape the desired form. There are many different turning techniques depending on your skill and comfort level and the object to be turned.

The work area should be set up with the tools needed for the kind of turning you wish to do. As well as basic shop tools you will need cutting tools such as gouges, scrapers, chisels, and parting tools which are selected for various functions (see photo below). Add various tool rests (see photo opposite) to aid cutting and a grinder for sharpening. Wood choice is also important and it's a good idea to collect suitable pieces to dry and have on hand. Exotic woods are expensive, but for laminated pattern work only a small quantity of any one wood is required so an exotic piece can add interest without too much expense. Many hobbyists build a wood collection over the years, storing it in the shop to dry sufficiently for working. It's important to find logs with interesting patterns and colors and these can vary depending on how you cut the wood. You may want to utilize the spalting to create additional interest. When the beauty of the wood is the central interest try to select a suitable form to best showcase this advantage. Finding woods to turn can lead to some fascinating discoveries. A walk in the woods often yields interesting fallen trees or branches that can be taken home. Another source is your own neighborhood when someone digs out a root or fells one of their trees. Neighbors are usually happy to save wood pieces for woodturners. Lumberyards are another source of wood and

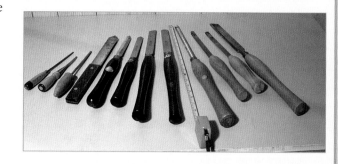

specialty shops stock exotic woods and will order in woods you choose. Also catalogues and woodworking magazines feature woods that you can order by mail or online.

◇ Safety

Safety is one of the most important elements of craft work and you should protect yourself from harm while you are making the projects. The use of power tools can be dangerous and care must be exercised when you use them. Working with wood has its own special hazards because some woods are toxic, especially if fine particles are breathed in. Also dull tools can cause accidents and can contribute to hazardous conditions. Cutting with a dull tool causes friction which generates heat and this can create fumes from the resins in the wood. These may be toxic and can cause mild to serious reactions. Avoid this with an air exchange system.

Tool Safety

1 Follow the manufacturer's suggestion on how to use the tool.

2 If tools have guards, leave them in place. Ground all electrical tools.

3 Wear safety glasses or a shield mask. Wear ear plugs.

4 Guide wood through blades with push sticks not fingers.

5 Sharp tools are safer to use. Keep tools in good repair.

6 Keep work area clean. Do not pile debris on tabletop.

7 Always stay alert when operating machinery. Turn tools off when not in use.

8 Do not clear saw tools with your hand. Unplug saw before cleaning, changing blades, or maintance work.

9 Wear proper clothing. Loose fitting clothes can get caught in machinery.

Dust Hazards

Turning wood creates sawdust and fine dust particles that can clog machinery and cause accidents. Fine dust when breathed in also causes serious respiratory problems as well as skin irritations. Man-made woods also present a problem because they contain chemicals, glues, and resins, even mold fungus that can be released into the air when the project wood is turned, cut, or sanded. Woods such as surinam, rosewood, redwood, mahogany, boxwood, satinwood, teak, ebony, wenge, and Western red elder contain an allergen called plicatic acid that can cause asthma. For protection against these hazards all woodturners should wear a mask (photo upper left). As well the workshop should be equipped with a good air filtration device and a dust collection system. Larger wood chips can be removed with a shovel and shop vacuum and do not pose the same threat. Safety glasses are also recommended to protect the eyes from airborne particles. Some new dust masks (photo above right) have replaceable electrostatic filters, a rubber face mask cup, and optional visor which provide good protection from dust particles, but it is always a good idea to capture fine particles at the source.

Work Area

It is important to keep the work area clean. This will improve safety and minimize the accumulation of dust particles.

1 Keep all cutting tools sharp to produce larger chips, less sawdust.

2 Do not over sand, clean the shop regularly to remove project dust.

3 Sometimes a scraper can replace a power sander and create less dust.

4 Keep unused tools stored away.

5 Have a separate place to store wood.

6 Vacuum shop area and wipe dusty machines and counters with a cloth.

7 It is always a good idea to test new woods before working with them.

8 Purchase tools with dust collector adapters.

9 Wear an apron when working and remove it before you leave the work areas. Wear closed toe shoes that can be left in the work area.

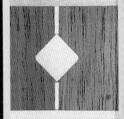

◇ Woods to Consider

Wood choice is important for the piece you are turning. Some woods turn more easily than others and may have distinctive grain patterns. Often heartwood and sapwood yield different colors and can be selected to enhance the project. Burls and spalting can also be used effectively for decorative interest.

Aburne This pale to light brown fine textured wood is sometimes streaked. Turns well.

African blackwood This wood turns well. Shades vary from purple-brown to black.

Alder This pale to light brown wood has dark streaking. Turns well.

American crab apple This wood is generally available and very decorative and easy to work with. It yields nearly white sapwood and almost walnut-brown heartwood.

Apple Fruit bearing trees yield very light sapwood and light brown heartwood. Turns well.

Arizona juniper Dull red wood similar to Western cedar. Can be highly figured with knots.

Ash White or American ash is most common and is easily worked. It has a yellowish-white color but does not cut across the grain.

Aspen Works well and has a whitish-yellow color but does not cut clean across the grain.

Basswood Creamy brown, fine textured wood, has straight grain.

Birch This wood has wavy grain patterns, spalts beautifully, and often grows spectacular burls. It can be almost iridescent when polished. Color varies from light yellow-brown to deep reddish-brown.

Black bean This imported wood is olive green with dark stripes.

Black locust A yellowish-brown wood which is very hard. Honey locust is creamier in color.

Bloodwood First choice for a deep, dark red color. Available at specialty stores. Also called cardinal wood.

Box elder This member of the soft maple family is prized by woodworkers because of the fungus-caused pink coloring, and often has a red-and-tan marble wood pattern.

Cedar (Northern white) This wood is commonly available, grows burls, and has elegant grain patterns.

Cedar (Western red) This straight-grained wood is commonly available, grows elegant burls, and is aromatic; however it is highly toxic and can cause serious health problems if dust is breathed in.

Ceylon ebony This imported wood is black interspersed with shades of brown, purple, and gray.

Chakte kok This wood is reddish with black streaks. The end grain has a swirl pattern.

Cherry This fine textured wood has reddish brown heartwood with brown flecks and lighter sapwood. American cherry is lighter than European cherry.

Cocobolo This member of the rosewood family buffs to a shiny finish, is durable, and maintains reddish color. The wood is safe but the sawdust if breathed in can cause a toxic shock reaction.

Courbaril Pale colored sapwood, reddish-brown heartwood, striped effect. Turns well.

Crystobal aspen Wood has reddish brown to violet heartwood, creamy sapwood. Also called granadillo.

Desert ironwood Dark brown hardwood. Turns well, produces high gloss polish.

Dymondwood (Colorwood) Man-made wood made of veneer, dyed red, green, or black under pressure, laminated into panels 36 in x 12 in x 3 in thick.

Ebony This imported wood is black interspersed with shades of brown, purple, and gray.

Gumwood This wood is often called satin walnut. It is milk brown, can be nicely marked.

Hackberry Of the elm family has yellow to grayish sapwood and yellowish gray-brown heartwood.

Harmdeam Dull white with gray stripes, even texture. Turns well.

Holly Commonly available, holly is the whitest known wood. Has a fine grain. Heartwood is cream-white, often with a greenish-gray cast, the sapwood is white or light tan. Black-dyed holly is sometimes sold as ebony.

Kingswood Violet brown wood with dark streaks. Turns well.

Laburnum This imported wood has a strong grain and rich olive green color.

Lacewood Light red colored wood with speckled or flaked appearance.

Lignum Wood is dark green with high oil content.

Laurel This imported wood is handsomely figured and is colored warm yellow to brown.

Magnolia Limited amount of wood harvested varies from green to reddish-brown.

Mahogany Commonly available, this wood is soft and works easily. It has deep brown to reddish color.

Maple There are many maples. Bird's Eye maple has bird's eye figuring and off-white color. Red maple has swirled grain patterns. Silver maple can be spalted, is off-white, and hard to finish. Sugar maple has elegant grain figures and is off-white, often with dark brown heart.

Moradillo This wood is reddish orange with darker red to brown streaks.

Mulberry (black and red) Commonly available, has a rich yellow color that darkens to golden brown.

Oak Many different varieties are available. The wood is many shades of brown with a distinctive grain.

Bog oak Having laid in water for 8000 years the tannin acid in the oak has turned wood black.

Osage orange This yellow wood turns orangy-brown when exposed to light.

Padauk This wood is reddish-purple, darkens to a deep reddish-purple or grayish-black on exposure.

8

Pau amarillo First choice wood for a bright canary yellow color. Available through specialty stores.

Pao rosa Wavy grain has pink, yellow, or dark brown heartwood often striped with red-brown bands.

Parallam Engineered beam 4 in x 12 in made of colored chips forming an attractive mosaic.

Pear This pale reddish yellow wood has a short close grain and is a favorite for carvers.

Pernambuco This imported quality hardwood is used in furniture making. It has a red color.

Pine Jack pine This wood is gray with interesting knots.

Pine Norfolk pine Creamy colored wood with dark gray area with copper colored circles.

Pine yellow pine Commonly available (or white pine), is soft but has interesting burls, crotches, and knots.

Pink ivory Fine textured bright pink wood producing beautiful polish.

Plum This nicely streaked wood is found in brownish or red.

Poplar This fine-textured whitish wood turns green or gray when exposed to light. Also called tulip tree.

Purpleheart This wood is light brown when cut but turns purple on exposure. Also called amarant.

Redwood This wood comes from farmed source and has a reddish color.

Rhododendron Shrubs often develop wood burls which make them interesting for woodworking.

Roots Lilac and majenta roots can be used for interesting effects.

Rosewood This beautiful imported wood is dark purple-brown banded with striped markings.

Red oak This coarse textured wood varies from light cream, pinkish red, to dark tan or brown.

Russian olive Wood is reddish brown, and has irregular growth, which may cause convoluted growth ring patterns.

Satinwood One of the most beautiful woods known, is brown with an overcast of salmon, green, gray, and sometimes black bindings. Imported.

Siberian elm This fairly brittle wood is a blend light brown color that can be used for contrast.

Snakewood (leopardwood) This dark brown wood has mottled spots. Rarely highly figured.

Staghorn sumac This "junk" plant has iridescent yellow-green wood that darkens slightly over time.

Swamp kauri Old New Zealand swamp wood, tan color, oily, lightly figured.

Sweet gum The sapwood is cream colored and the heartwood (commercially sold as American red green) varies from a satiny pinkish-brown to a deep red-brown.

Sycamore This imported wood is nearly milk-white and often richly mottled.

Taun Pale brown wood with pink tinge and wavy grain.

Tulipwood Hard dense wood has pinkish to yellowish heartwood with violet, salmon, and rose stripes.

Tupelo This wood has interlocked grain with gray-brown sapwood and darker heartwood.

Ulmo (Chilean honey tree) Deep rosy red wood with even grain. Easily worked.

Walnut Varies from tan to purple-brown/black (coarse texture but sands to a smooth satin finish).

Wenge The heartwood is dark brown with fine black veins and white lines. It has a straight grain.

Yellow willow This soft wood is a pale yellowish-gray color.

Yew Heartwood is orange-brown to golden-orange, purple and brown streaks. Irregular grain pattern.

Zebra wood Heartwood has brown stripes running through creamy yellowish background. Wood is stinky so wear a mask when working the wood. Imported from Africa.

Man-Made Wood

Some interesting pieces can be made with man-made woods. *Dymondwood* is made from ¹⁄₁₆ in veneers (or thinner) of hardwoods that are vacuum impregnated with dye and phenolic resin. It comes in over 20 different colors or multicolors in dimensions of 2 ½ in thick x 12 in wide x 36 in long. *Colorwood* is a wood laminate of natural and brightly dyed northern hardwood veneers in various color configurations. It is excellent for unique, colorful items such as pens, rolling pins, bowls, etc. These woods are very stable and will not twist or warp. They finish well. Dymondwood and Colorwood can also be used for an accent piece, in special designs.

Colorwood Dymondwood

Parallam wood bowl

Resin molds

Resin goblet

Resin bowl shaped on lathe

9

Another man-made material known as *Parallam* beams is manufactured from long thin strands of wood bonded together in a patented microwave process. The beams come in various dimensions. Portions of these beams can be used to turn bowls and vases. Turning this wood produces a mosaic of patterns of various colors. Resin is another man-made material that can be used for novelty turning. Although it is not wood it can be enhanced with wood sawdust to add interest and color. This 2-component epoxy can be shaped the same way as wood. Polymer clays can also be turned.

In recent years a product called Pentacryl has become available that is designed to help prevent cracks and checks in green wood. This viscous liquid quickly migrates into wet wood, displacing its natural moisture so the wood won't crack. Some green wood has different levels of moisture in the sapwood, heartwood, and knots. When it is air dried or even kiln dried, cracks can still develop internally. A Pentacryl treatment can help prevent this from happening. The product is easy to use and produces good results. Simply brush it on liberally on a turned piece that is ½ in thick. Coat on both sides and allow to stand for 24 hours. Then finish turning.

This vase is green Norfolk pine. Pentacryl treatment gives slight yellow color

Wood Grain

To locate the center of stock use a square or ruler and mark clearly. When turning with the grain where the wood piece is long and the end grain is not worked, screws will not hold in the end grain so drive is effected through a spur. The other end of the project is supported by the tailstock with revolving center. When the grain runs across the object's surface, cut the wood as round as possible with a band saw and attach with screws to the faceplate. If you do not wish to use screws in the project use a piece of scrap wood thick enough to hold the screws, glue wrapping paper between project wood and scrap wood and remove later by splitting at paper location with a chisel.

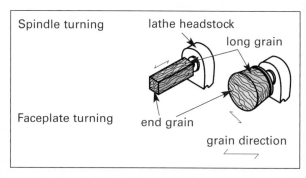

Spindle turning — lathe headstock — long grain

Faceplate turning — end grain — grain direction

◇ *Wood Seasoning*

Since all species of wood can be turned it is important to make them as suitable as possible. Seasoning removes sap and water so turned wood won't shrink, warp, or have open joints. Large wood pieces can be stacked on skids in the open air and allowed to dry away from direct sunlight and water. This takes one year drying time for every inch thickness of wood. Kiln drying is also an option. However, many turners choose green turning for bowls to make a bowl blank which is then allowed to dry, finding its own shape. Since shrinkage is not uniform the shape may warp but can be corrected at the later turning. Cracks may also appear from unequal shrinkage and these can affect turning or make the piece useless. To help prevent cracking wrap piece in a few layers of newspaper to slow the drying.

It's a good idea to do centerwork turning such as boxes, candle holders, eggcups and faceplate turning of cuttingboards and plates from dry wood so they won't warp. Deep bowls, however, are easier to turn from green wood, then dried before they are finished.

◇ *Tools*

For woodturners the essential tool is the lathe and the choice on the market today is limitless. Professional or commercial turners can use high-tec models to make intricate turning a simple operation. Craftsmen and hobbyists, however don't require such complex machines. While a very basic machine can be purchased for two to five hundred dollars, an adequate lathe for woodturning costs less than a thousand dollars. The choice of machine depends on the work you plan to do. There are free-standing and bench-style lathes. Whichever you choose it should be installed in your workplace so that vibration is limited. Think of a cast iron bed or some means of fixing to the floor. Height is important for

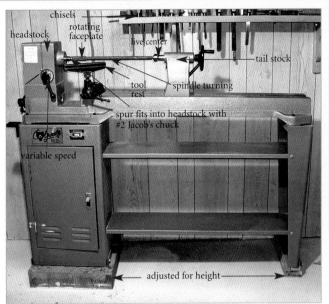

ease of working. The lathe can be adjusted for height so that the center is 2 to 3 inches above your elbow. Traditionally the headstock is on the left and the tailstock is on the right. Make sure there is enough room to work freely at the end of the lathe. Look for quick change variable speed and a good distance between center and swing-over bed. This determines the maximum diameter that can be turned on the lathe.

An easy-to-change tool rest is helpful and should be positioned about ⅛ in from the work so that the wood turns clear of it. Wood is turned with or across the grain and turning tools are designed to cut or scrape to accommodate these needs. Use a *gouge* for turning with the grain to shave the chosen wood from square to round, use a *skew chisel* to make a smooth cut for center work, use a *parting tool* to cut off the project from the discard wood, and use a *round-nosed chisel* ground on one side to scrape out wood for hollowing. For turning across the grain use d*eep-fluted gouges* from large to small size and finish with a *grind gouge* for corners. Use *scrapers* for final smoothing. A variety of measuring tools is needed. To locate the center of the stock use a square or ruler and mark clearly.

A variety of tool rests is needed for spindle shaping and for the inside and outside shaping of bowls and vases. Attaching a project to a faceplate is usually done by a center screw (more screws for heavier pieces). The tail center can be used with the faceplate to provide extra support. The Jacob's chuck is used to grip thin projects and three-jaw and four-jaw chucks can grip irregular shapes. Many turners use spigot chucks (good for small plates & bowls) or jam-fit chucks which work very well and provide a friction fit.

Most turners make preliminary drawings of the proposed object before they begin turning, first studying the grain pattern before the shaping begins. Over the years the turner learns when to stop and when the piece looks right. From experience turners learn tool-handling techniques that produce the best results for them. Sometimes chisels have to be shaped to make an intricate cut. Sharp chisels work best. In fact, it's a good idea to have a grindstone nearby to keep touching up the edge, especially for hardwoods.

Patterned objects require more preparation and usually a drawing or layout of the different kinds of wood and where it will be placed to make the required designs. The different wood pieces are measured, cut, and laminated with yellow glue to assemble. Experience and patience are the turner's greatest allies as he strives to master the craft. Experimenting with tools and altering them for certain procedures can lead to new techniques.

◇ *Measuring*

Although woodturners value spontaneity in their turning and judge distances by eye, sometimes precise measurements are required and a few basic measuring tools should be part of your shop equipment. Include a set of calipers, dividers, and rulers. Measuring is important when turning chair legs or fitting lids to boxes, and vital when making laminated patterns. Also centering the project work on the lathe should be carefully calculated. This not only reduces vibration but also ensures balance for the finished piece and keeps the spinning wood from flying off the lathe.

◇ *Tool Sharpening*

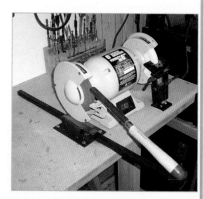

Sharp tools are absolutely essential and may be the most important aspect for successful woodturning. The quality of the edge depends on the tool you are using and the kind of wood being turned. Many turners find that the best way to remove a large amount of wood quickly is to grind the cutting tool. Grinding can produce a keen enough edge for woodturning and can be done often and quickly enough to be practical for tools that dull quickly doing woodturning work. A grinder with 36-grit and 80-grit carborundum wheels works well. There are several types of grinders on the market. Choose the best you can afford. The object of grinding is to produce a single-facet bevel. Grind out large chips on the coarse wheel and finish on the finer wheel. Do not grind so long that the tool overheats. If it turns blue dip it in water to cool it. If a burr exists after grinding it can be removed with a slipstone lubricated with a light machine oil or on a bench stone. Woodturning tools need to be sharpened very often and woodturners usually have the grindstone close by. There are many books devoted to proper grinding procedures.

◇ *Basic Procedure*

Making a Box and Lid

To make a simple cylindrical base and lid, for example, requires attaching the chosen wood (here Norfolk pine) to the lathe and turning to a cylindrical shape. Choose a log 18 in long by 6 in diameter. This tree, native to Hawaii, has striking color with red knots, which make effective decoration (see photo 1). Cut off a 7 in section.

Hold between the spur at the headstock and the live center at the tailstock. Round off with chisel and true up the ends. (see photo 2).

To make sure the piece is securely attached to the faceplate, use a backing piece fastened to the faceplate with screws (photo 3). Then recess the backing piece ¼ in to accept the rounded log for the base of the bowl. Glue (yellow glue) the section into this recess.

Now use a narrow parting tool to cut a top and bottom of matching grain. Cut off 2 ½ in from the other end of the log. In a similar way attach this piece to a second faceplate prepared in like manner. You can mount and remove these faceplates from the lathe repeatedly and the work will remain true and balanced. Make sure that the top of the box and the bottom of the lid retain the same position to match the grain (see photo 4).

Hollow out the inside of the box with a skew chisel (see photo 5). Switch faceplates at the headstock and hollow out the inside of the lid with a skew chisel (see photo 6). Separate the lid from its faceplate with the narrow parting tool. The lid should fit snugly on the box. Carefully sand the joint where the lid meets the box and also the top of the lid which is slightly convex (see photo 7). With the parting tool separate the box from its faceplate (see photo 8). The box and lid are complete and await finishing (see photo 9). Choose a varnish for the box and lid (see photo 10).

Tapered Vase and Lid

This matching tapered vase was made from the same piece of wood (see photo 1) as the box and lid. Cut off a piece 9 ½ in long. Turn the log to round it off (see photo 11) and cut both ends back 1 in leaving a centered piece 1 in diameter to fit the block screwed to the faceplate.

For lidded vases use 2 faceplates. Cut 1 in holes in the center of blocks on the faceplates to fit rounded log ends. Glue one faceplate at each end of log and allow to dry 24 hours. Mount on lathe at headstock and live center on tailstock (see photo 12). This way you can switch the ends around or take them off and put on again and still maintain the balance. Rough shape the vase.

Allow 5 ½ in for body of vase (see photo 13), 1 ½ in for base, 1 ½ in from edge of lid to the top of the knob. Use thin parting tool to separate lid from main body, leaving body 4 ½ in high and 1 in for lid portion. The vase has straight tapers. The top ledge on lid is 5 in diameter. Base of bowl is 3 ¼ in diameter, with matching taper.

With lid removed, hollow out vase (see photo 14) with chisel leaving sides ¼ in thick. Place lid faceplate on headstock (see photo 15). Cut a lip ⅜ in to fit inside vase, so veins in wood match. Hollow out inside center of lid (see photo 16).

13

17

Replace main faceplate back on headstock and lid faceplate on tailstock. With pressure on tailstock this again turns as one unit. Finish the unit carefully to maintain sharp edges. Use fine parting tool to separate project from faceplates to within ½ in. Cut this with a hacksaw and complete with a sander.

Vase is 8 in tall. Finish the same way as Box and Lid. Both projects made by John Hiebert (see photo 17).

Turning Techniques

Plain woodturning begins and ends with a single piece of wood. The beauty of the finished piece depends on proportion and scale judged through the eye of the turner. Wood choice including color, grain pattern, knots, and burls dictates the final form of the design which evolves during the turning. This type of turning can produce a vast array of creative styles that can be utilitarian or entirely decorative. The technique emphasizes the beauty of the wood and illustrates the combination of wood and form to create art.

When making a patterned project the wood chosen is important for the pattern, color, and design. This can be achieved by gluing together strips or sheets of different woods to form colored layers (see photo 18). How you laminate the sheets is determined by what you want to achieve. Different thicknesses of wood, different colors, or different angles can produce an endless opportunity to create a variety of patterns. A more complex construction is stacked lamination which features many layers of wood glued together one on top of the other. Within this stack, patterns can be built in or a design or pattern can be incorporated that is revealed as the wood is turned. There are many suitable glues to do this work. Generally, yellow glue is recommended.

18

If the wood pieces or segments are glued together in a predetermined pattern and assembled to the desired form this involves patience and skill. The individual segments can vary in size and number to make up the design which can be fairly complex. The cuts must be precise and the seams as invisible as possible. Some designs involve thousands of wood segments and must be mathematically measured and calculated in order for the design to take shape.

Another aspect of woodturning is joinery. When parts of the project are turned separately this allows for much detailed work such as carving, cut out work, burning, inlaying, and painting to be done on the separate pieces, which are then joined to produce the final object.

14

◇ *Finishing*

Norfolk pine vase, rough turned green, treated with Pentacryl (gives a golden coat) & immediately finish - turned & sprayed with Varathane

Choice of finishing depends on the wood and the future use of the woodturned object keeping in mind that you want the beauty of the natural wood to be enhanced. Begin with sanding. Sanding is very important and various grades of garnet papers (80,100, 180 grit) and even 220 and 280 grit are used for extra smoothness. Each progressive grit removes the scratches left behind from the previous grit. Going beyond 280 grit will close the grain and not allow the finish to penetrate properly. When the finish is applied to the project you can then use finer grits, up to 600 grit and beyond, between coats. You can also use these finer grit papers with a lubricant for a final polish. Garnet sandpaper is a natural abrasive and produces a smooth finish, whether applied by hand or when object is turning on a machine. Most woodworkers choose open coat sandpaper which has gaps between the grits to give the sawdust somewhere to go, preventing clogging. Closed coat clogs quickly and is best used for metal finishing.

Candlestick's intricate design is finished with spray-on oil-based varnish

Bloodwood and maple bowl hand polished with twelve coats of lacquer-based Turner's polish while lathe is spinning

Some ornamental pieces can be finished with varnish, Varathane, or Polyurethane to give a hard, bright sheen but others look better with a softer finish such as mineral oil or beeswax. If a piece is oiled it takes about 2 to 3 weeks of oiling process to bring out the translucence of the wood. This happens as the oil penetrates the cell spaces in the wood that were formerly filled with water. The result is a plastic like finish. Spraying with chemicals is not a good idea. Glass cleaner will permanently etch the finish. Direct sunlight will damage the finish and the wood and sometimes causes the wood to change color.

If you are making a utilitarian piece such as bowls, candy dishes, etc. do not finish with walnut oil or peanut oil. These can infiltrate the object's contents and cause severe allergic reactions for some people. Better to use finishes that are food safe (please check internet). To maintain the finish on a non functional piece apply a light coat of fine furniture paste wax with a soft cloth. Dry and buff. Wash utility pieces by hand with soap and water, then rinse and dry immediately with a soft towel. Do not soak bowls in water or allow them to stand for any length of time with liquid or left-over food inside the bowl. It's best to use non-scratching utensils.

Oak and cherry goblet finished with Danish oil which dries to a hard finish. Popular easy finish. Apply more coats for a harder finish

Maple vase is finished in teak oil

15

Henry Bergen

I grew up on the Ukrainian Steppes where wood was a scarce commodity. When I was 4 or 5 I found a stick and I wanted to make a whip handle for my pretend wild stallions. My siblings wouldn't help me but Dad did. The carved handle was perfect and I learned that even a scrap of wood can be made into something beautiful. That is how my love of wood began and it is my interest to this day.

My approach to woodturning is quite simple. What interests me most is the wood itself - the grain, the texture, the shape of a particular log. If my neighbor fells a tree or digs up a root and gives it to me I work directly with the green wood, often when it is very wet. I hardly ever purchase lumber. This makes my hobby inexpensive and I can afford to experiment.

I take my time with a piece of wood to bring out the best grain pattern and I take great pleasure in watching the rope-like shavings accumulate on my work bench as I visualize what the log wants to be. I never glue up any wood to make bigger objects. I have developed my own techniques of turning. I start with green wood and rough out the bowl or vase form, leaving enough extra for shrinkage as it dries. I allow the rough blank to air dry, sometimes for months, before I begin my final turning. I've found that it's a good idea to coat the blanks with wax or wrap them in newspaper to slow the drying process, and to prevent uneven drying, the cause of splitting. Sometimes a knot or burl will influence the shaping and I may leave part of the bark for effect. I try to take advantage of every aspect of the wood for my creations. Since I never know what's under the bark of the log when I start, turning is full of surprises and that keeps me excited and interested.

I make many projects simply for the love of creating them and I take them to judged woodworking shows where I can talk to other turners. I now sell some of my finished pieces.

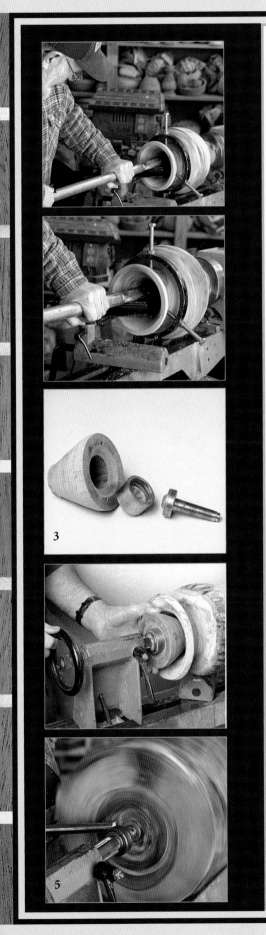

3

5

Turning Vases

Turning vases is one of the most enjoyable things I do. I must have made hundreds, each with a separate problem. Here are a few tips I've learned that may suit you. I've converted my garage into a workshop where I've installed an inexpensive lathe which I find adequate for my hobby woodturning. I began with standard lathe tools but since I make mostly large bowls and vases, I found the tools too short for the depths I needed to excavate large deep projects. Over time a friend helped me solve the problem. He took a 10 in long, 1 in steel bar and cut a 2 in long x ³⁄₁₆ in deep slot in one end, which he fitted with 2 set screws to provide seating for a variety of cutting bits. He welded a 3 ft length of pipe to this and I had a 4-ft-long tool that was long enough for my ambitions (see photo 1).

Another problem was a chuck that had trouble holding the project pieces against even a slight catch of the chisel. And because of the distance of the cutting chisel from the chuck, the project invariably began to judder and was knocked off center before I could react. Another friend helped me out. He made a stabilizing yoke (see photo 2) consisting of a 12 x 20 mm steel ring with 3 equally spaced, threaded bolt holes drilled through it. The ring has the diameter of the neck of the largest bowl you wish to turn. It is welded to a mount that fits the lathe so the center of the ring aligns with the center of the lathe. Bolts that are rounded and polished at the tips screw into the holes and are kept in place against vibration by extra nuts. The bolts are tightened snug to the project piece. This works perfectly for me. Commercial stabilizing devices are available in the metal machining industry and you may be able to adjust them to serve your needs or you can make mine.

Finally, another problem is associated with working the exterior for the finish cut. While drying, the wood will warp and acquire mildew and dust discoloration. And wood gouges may be evident from the bolts. The exterior needs to be reshaped, but since the yoke can't be used another stabilization method is needed. My friend milled a steel cone to fit over a tail stock live center for small projects (see photo 3) and I turned an oak cone to fit over the steel cone for larger projects (see photo 4). When you mount the project in the chuck at the drive end with the vase open mouth to the tail stock, the cone fits snugly into the vase and keeps it steady during cutting. Photo 5 shows the end cut off the log to expose the color so the turner can have some idea of what is hidden under the bark to decide how to shape the pieces.

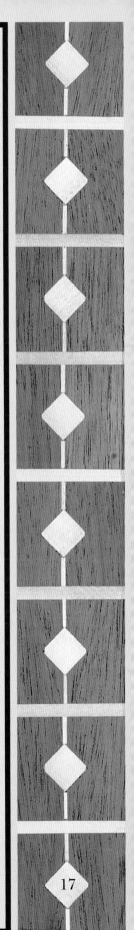

Maple Vase

1 Maple produces brilliantly colored foliage every fall, the result of fungal decay of the sap. That same process may occur in the wood itself when a tree dies, sometimes giving the wood a bright red tinge, such as the vase at

right or the maple plate below the vase. In the piece of log I used, the heart was already punky, which can make the centers work loose and shift. I insert steel washers between the spur center at the head, the live center at the tail, and the log to help prevent this (see photo 6).

2 Work the exterior roughly to the desired shape. A vase neck, besides giving shape to the piece, is useful for accommodating a running track for the circle yoke bolts (see photo 7). Provide a stub at the bottom end of the vase to mount in the chuck when working inside the vase.

3 With a parting tool, cut a groove at the base of the vase leaving enough wood to support the work for finishing. (Note As cracking usually begins at the ends of logs, the groove will help prevent cracks that develop in the stub from spreading into the vase base).

4 Hollow out vase. (Note Wood shrinks as it dries, and uneven removal of the inside mass will result in uneven drying and probable cracking. I have ruined a number of my more promising pieces by not removing enough of the internal wood bulk).

Maple vase featuring bark and fungal decay

5 Remove headstock spur center and install a common chuck.

6 Except for smaller vases, you will probably need the circle yoke to support the vase when gouging out the inside to prevent a catching tool from knocking the vase off balance (see photo 7).

Maple bowl incorporating split and fungus (face view) and turned to leave bark trim on the edges (side view).

Mount the project in the chuck and balance it using the tailstock and cones to align the piece in its previous position. Trim away any off-round wood at the narrowest part of the neck for the circle yoke bolts. Align the yoke with that spot.

Balancing Logs

Since I use mainly unprocessed wood the logs are irregular and difficult to balance on the lathe. It helps when you begin to run the empty lathe at high speed, stop, then turn the lever to the lowest speed. This disengages the drive from the motor and allows the spindle to turn more freely for balancing. Position the log between headstock and tailstock and rotate by hand to test for weight distribution and reposition until the log does not turn on its own. You'll probably need a live tailstock center for satisfactory balance unless your lathe is heavy enough to withstand imbalance judder. A dead center will bind too much to allow sufficient torque sensitivity for a project piece that is off balance. Setting both ends off-center in the opposite direction will keep the log balanced but allow sapwoods and heartwoods to show in different patterns and expose knots and burls that can be incorporated into the design.

Tighten the bolts snug to the project. Note   For smoother operation, lubricate running track of bolts with beeswax which is used by the Dutch to lubricate large wooden gears in windmills (very effective).

7   Gouge out inside of the vase (see photo 8). This can be speeded up by using Forstner/saw-tooth bits on a drill chuck mounted on the tailstock. Unless the wood is very irregular, leave ½ in to ¾ in thickness at the first cut.

8   Remove work piece and wrap it in three to five layers of newspaper, to slow the drying process, prevent cracking, and avoid sweating that causes fungus growth. If the bark is to be left on the project, it is critical that decay of the cambium be prevented so the bark won't loosen. After 2 to 3 months, the piece should be dry enough for final cutting. Judge the moisture by the 'feel' of the covering paper.

9   To finish the project, remount the piece in the chuck and install the end cone. Shape the piece to desired form and sand. I use a flexible sanding disk with a hand drill while the lathe is running. This method helps smooth out curves and ridges. Depending on the condition of the cut surface, progress from coarse to fine grit (60, 120, 180, 220, 280 grit paper). The last bit of sanding is always done by hand. For especially fine-grained wood, such as crab apple, use 320 grit or higher.

10   Cut off the stub. For finishing I use teak oil which penetrates well into the wood, bark, and crevices without leaving a layer of oil on the surface. On especially smooth pieces, without flaws and nuances, I may use Turner's polish for a better shine.

11   When bark has dried out too much before processing the log it may develop a frayed look, or the wood may develop cracks and weak spots where decay has progressed too far. To stabilize the fibers, use a diluted solution of yellow glue and detergent. Continually brush it on until the piece is well saturated. Let it dry 2 or 3 days before finishing. The detergent solution has no staining or other effects on the wood. Commercial products are available but they are expensive and don't offer any better results.

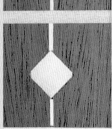

19

Vase Variations

Once the log is secured between headstock and tailstock, the outer shape of the vase can be determined by the cutting chisel and the condition of the log. Different woods and figuration of knots and burls suggest varying shapes.

Crab apple vase had its shape determined by heartwood, sapwood, and bark

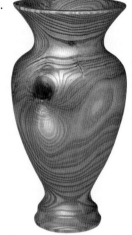

Russian olive vase utilizes unusual grain pattern for interest

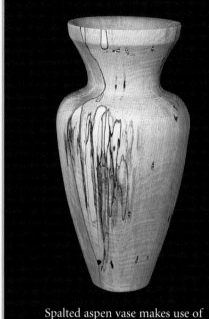

Spalted aspen vase makes use of fungus as decoration

Turning bowls

Basically there are only two ways to approach a log: end-on or sideways at various angles or off center (see diagram p10 and below). Each has advantages, disadvantages, and unique characteristics. End-on bowls are simplest and easiest, offering the least challenge – and the least interesting result I might add – unless they have special features such as cracks or burls (see photo 9). Sideways bowls are more difficult to finish because end grain is difficult to smooth out. Not only do bark and knots offer diversion but grain, fungus, and insect damage may also prove interesting. Using a forked log is another interesting possibility (see photo 10). When the fungus causes the wood to fall apart in an interesting piece being turned, the bowl can still be salvaged. In this case I made a false bottom to replace the rotten wood. See p21.

9

Elm log with interesting burl pattern

10

Elm forked log using side cut

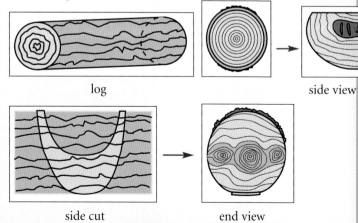

log

side view

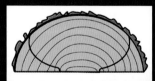

perpendicular grain

side cut

end view

end grain view

Maple bowl with false bottom

Elm side cut caravel shape bowl, showing working stub

Rough cut caravel bowl

Dowel plugs in bowls

Aspen bowl with partial bark trim

Russian olive bowl with natural surface convolution

Aspen Bowl

1 Choose a log and cut off a length to suit the depth of the bowl desired, adding 2 in for the mounting stub.

2 Clamp the log between tailstock and headstock and balance as for vases. Square off the top end of the bowl project and check for rim suitability. A pencil held against the wood near the edge will give an idea how much wood and/or bark needs to be removed. Logs are seldom evenly round. Later, by repeatedly removing wood and moving the center, it will be possible to choose how much wood to expose on the outer edge of the bowl and how much bark to leave. Care should be taken that enough wood remains all around to support any bark remaining without making the piece too bulky. Also, if the bowl wall curves outward from the rim, care must be taken that the wood is not cut through to the bark from the inside at any point as this will preclude a smooth finish for the inside of the bowl and cause uneven warping and weakness.

3 I usually first work the piece to its desired shape from the outside. Then I hollow out accordingly. Depending on the depth, the inside can be carved out while mounted between headstock and tailstock (spindle turning) without changing to chuck mounting. This helps prevent the piece breaking loose if a chisel catches, and it allows the use of greater chisel pressure.

4 Try to avoid sharp curves on the inside of the bowl which may leave tool marks that will be difficult to sand out. Note Carving and sanding end-on bowl bottoms are problematic because that is perpendicular to the grain.

Russian Olive Bowl

1 Of more interest and greater possibilities are the side cut bowls (bottom left). The Russian olive log was cut shorter and corners removed to fit my 12 in lathe.

2 Clamp between headstock and tailstock, with the grain and lathe axis perpendicular. Cut away wood to near its final shape. Here, growth rings showed interesting patterns. I left part of the irregular growth of the tree fork at the rim of the bowl. Note Irregularities could be removed, making the bowl shallower, or more could be included making the bowl deeper.

3 Since wood has a tendency to develop cracks at the heart, to help prevent this I squared off the piece for the rim of the bowl through the heart of one of the branches, leaving a stub inside the bowl for the tailstock center. This left a fairly open bowl to be hollowed out without remounting. Leave the stub fairly substantial until the rough cut is finished and then whittle it down at the bottom end until it is easily broken off.

4 Wrap the piece in paper and set aside to dry.

5 I did not have enough wood at the bottom of the bowl to leave a stub for chuck-mounting, so with a parting tool, I

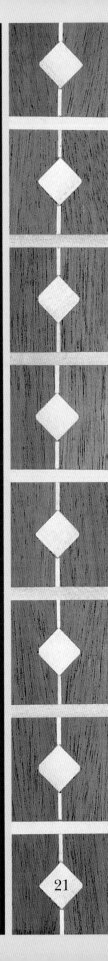

21

squared off the bottom, leaving a small stub from the spur center.

6 Using the spur center mark, I drilled a hole (the size of the central hole of the faceplate) into bottom of the bowl.

7 Remove the stub and glue a short piece of dowel into the hole (see photo p21). Heat up the faceplate and melt some glue-gun glue onto the plate. Use a dowel plug to keep the faceplate centered, and adhere the plate to the bottom of the bowl.

8 When cool, turn the faceplate onto the spindle and the bowl is ready for finishing.

9 This method of fastening has an advantage over screws which might tear loose. The faceplate is easily removed by reheating. Scrape and sand off glue.

Candleholders

1 Burl has unique internal and surface grain structure, and some examples are large enough to incorporate in bowls and vases. If you look for unusual shapes you can find two burls to make simple, yet unique, candleholders.

2 Mount the wood piece between the headstock and tailstock and turn to desired shape.

3 Square off at heart end of the piece, leaving the spines to show.

4 Glue endplate to bottom (as for Russian olive bowl) and mount the piece on the lathe.

5 Drill desired size hole with a bit held in a chuck supported in the tailstock.

6 Clean out dead bark from the rough burl surface with nylon fiber brush wheel in a hand drill.

Here (see photo 12), a wide supporting base for a taller holder was not possible because the usable wood got narrower towards the center of the tree trunk (this pair was made from the outer layer of a dying maple). I made the holders shorter and bulkier to provide enough support for the candles and the project became a tea candleholder.

Caragana is a hedge shrub and grows only up to 4 in diameter stalk, which limits the pieces that can be made. The wood has a very dense fiber structure, is easy to work, and finishes beautifully. The heart of caragana is an attractive brown and the outer layer a yellowish white creating a pleasing distinct contrast. I've used it to make these candle holders and a small rose vase providing bases from other material, in this case aspen (see photo on p23). I inserted a small glass vial in the vase so that it can be used for a fresh-cut flower. Small toothpick holder is also from caragana.

22

Maple Bowl

1 Maple is interesting for bowls but its use has some problems. Older, interesting trees with punky wood often cannot be used. To save this wood piece, I reversed the piece on the chuck and reamed out the bottom center to solid wood.

2 Turn a plug of similar wood to fit the hole and glue into the base (see photo top p 21). Finish the same as Russian olive bowl.

3 Finish the inner surface with food-safe oil since this bowl is intended for practical use.

4 Another interesting side cut maple bowl is shown in photo 11.

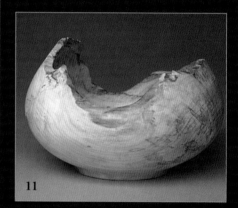

11

12

23

John Hiebert

I'm sure every woodturner has a passion for wood and I am one of these people. I remember working on construction crews when I was a young man, following a particular finishing craftsman around to watch and learn. He always managed to show the wood to its best advantage and that impressed me. Years later, when I set up my own workshop, a radial arm saw was the first tool I purchased so I could build cupboards and furniture that my wife and I needed for our new house. Gradually I ventured to work with exotic hardwoods and my first endeavor was a small table made from purpleheart. I designed it myself. I learned that I could look at a piece of wood and visualize its finished form. This was exciting and led to many wood adventures.

When I bought a lathe and began woodturning the art of the craft seemed unlimited in its scope. Turning different woods together fascinated me and I created patterns as new ideas came to me. Laminating allowed me to combine exotic woods and colors to express designs that I admired, in particular the blankets and baskets of people of the Southwest and other geometric patterns they used.

Woodturning is a hobby for me and I pursue it with great enthusiasm. I am able to make a variety of turned wood projects with a selection of good tools. Besides regular shop tools I have a fairly expensive lathe with a selection of chisels, set of faceplates, tool rests, a thickness planer, a grinder, and a drill press miter saw for cutting angles and I treat myself to a few specialty tools from time to time. I collect exotic woods and I usually have a variety of more common wood pieces on hand that are dry and ready for use. I purchase other woods locally as I need them. I enjoy entering woodworking shows which are always instructive. My pieces are popular gifts for family and friends.

Pink Rolling Pin

Material
Dymondwood 18 ½ in x 2 ⁹⁄₁₆ in x 2 ¹¹⁄₁₆ in

Procedure

1 A quick and easy way to make an attractive rolling pin is by using Dymondwood (see photo 1), which is widely available from suppliers of exotic woods. It comes in varying lengths, widths, and thicknesses.

2 Use the calipers to determine the exact center of the ends of piece for the spur point and the live center point. Set calipers just under the half of the narrowest side and make a pencil mark from all 4 sides (if calipers are set a little under or a little over it doesn't matter (see photo 2). This makes a small square (see photo 2). Punch a hole in the center of this square with an awl.

3 Center the block on the lathe (see photo 3). Turn the main body of the rolling pin down to 2 ½ in diameter and 11 in long. Turn both ends 3 ¼ in with the outside diameter 1 ¾ in tapering down to 1 ¼ in. The space between the body and the knob is 1 in and 1 in diameter.

4 Turned rolling pin is ready for sanding.

5 Finish with five coats of high gloss Varathane.

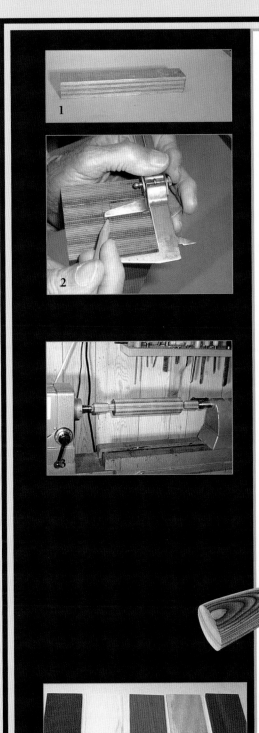

Striped Rolling Pin

Material
Bloodwood 24 in x 3 ⅛ in
Ulmo (Chilean honey tree) 24 in x 3 ⅛ in
Pau amarillo 24 in x 3 ⅛ in
Purpleheart 24 in x 3 ⅛ in
Maple 24 in x 3 ⅛ in
Stack wood from top to bottom in order listed.

Procedure

1 Stack wood lengths as directed. Cut pieces in half and use the 2 halves, one on either side of the center piece which is bloodwood (see photo 1).

Left to right all pieces varying in thicknesses 3 ⅛ in x 24 in purpleheart, maple, ulmo (Chilian honey tree) pau amarillo, bloodwood

25

2 Draw the outside dimensions of the finished rolling pin on a piece of gluing board template: total length 17 ½ in, main body 11 in x 2 ⅞ in, past each end of main body 3 ¼ in x 1 ¾ in (see photo 2). Draw a line diagonally to place the first piece (bloodwood, see photo 3). With an awl mark the center top edge of wood at 3 in and 11 in to correspond with template, for future reference point.

3 Begin gluing wood pieces with yellow carpenter's glue to first bloodwood piece (see photo 4).

4 When gluing up from the central bloodwood use half of the 24 in boards that you cut in half on one side and the other half on the other side to ensure that both sides are identical (see photo 5).

5 Block is made when pieces are glued together.

6 With the square at reference points 3 and 11 on the bloodwood, draw a continuing line on the top of both sides of the block (see photo 6). Fill in the lines on the gluing board.

7 Continue the lines as you progress with the gluing. Once the main body is made it is not necessary that the outside lines be fully covered. (see photo 7)

8 The pencil lines show where the ends of the main body will come (see photo 8). The glue-up is now complete (see photo 9).

9 On the band saw trim each side of the block to the pencil line (see photo 10). Trim the ends of the block so there is 4 in on each end past the end of the main body. This gives a solid center to mount on the lathe.

10 Using the thickness planer, shave the top and bottom of the block down to 3 in. The sides of the block should also be down to 3 in, making a 3 in square, still showing the reference points in the center of the bloodwood (see photo 11).

11 When turning on the lathe keep ⅛ in away from pencil marks that show the end of the main body of rolling pin to allow for any adjustments. Turn down to 2 ⅞ in (see photo 12).

12 To achieve a mirror image trim right end back,

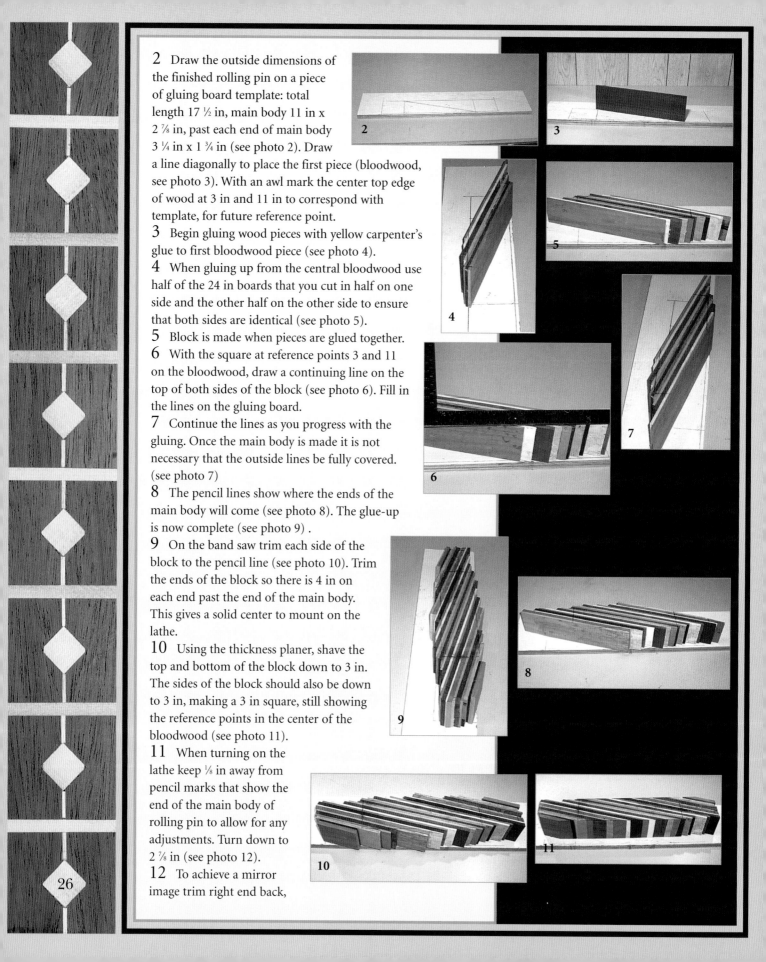

26

cutting ⅛ in off end of bloodwood of the main body
(see photo 13).

13 Give the block one half rotation and repeat the process for the spur end (see photo 14).

14 Now turn ends that extend 3 ¼ in past the main body. Turn knobs to 1 ¾ in diameter at the outside tapering down to 1 ¼ in. There is 1 in space between knob and body. This part has 1 in diameter (see photo 15).

15 Partially cut off handle with a parting tool (see photo 15).

16 After removing the rolling pin from the lathe trim off the ends on band saw. Smooth with sander.

17 Finish with 5 coats of high gloss Varathane.

Thunderbird
Rolling Pin & Cutting Board

Material
Bloodwood ¾ in x 1 ½ in x 48 in long
Maple ¾ in x 1 ½ in x 48 in long
Ulmo ¾ in x 1 ½ in x 48 in long
Satinwood ¾ in x 1 ½ in x 48 in long
Purpleheart ¾ in x 1 ½ in x 48 in long
Pink Dymondwood ¾ in x 1 ½ in x 3 ½ in long

Procedure
1 The feathered arrow section and the thunderbird section are similar in the rolling pin and cutting board and can be made at the same time.

2 Prepare material for the feathers of feathered arrow section. Use boards ¾ in thick by 48 in long and rip strips 1 ½ in wide on a radial arm saw (see photo 1).

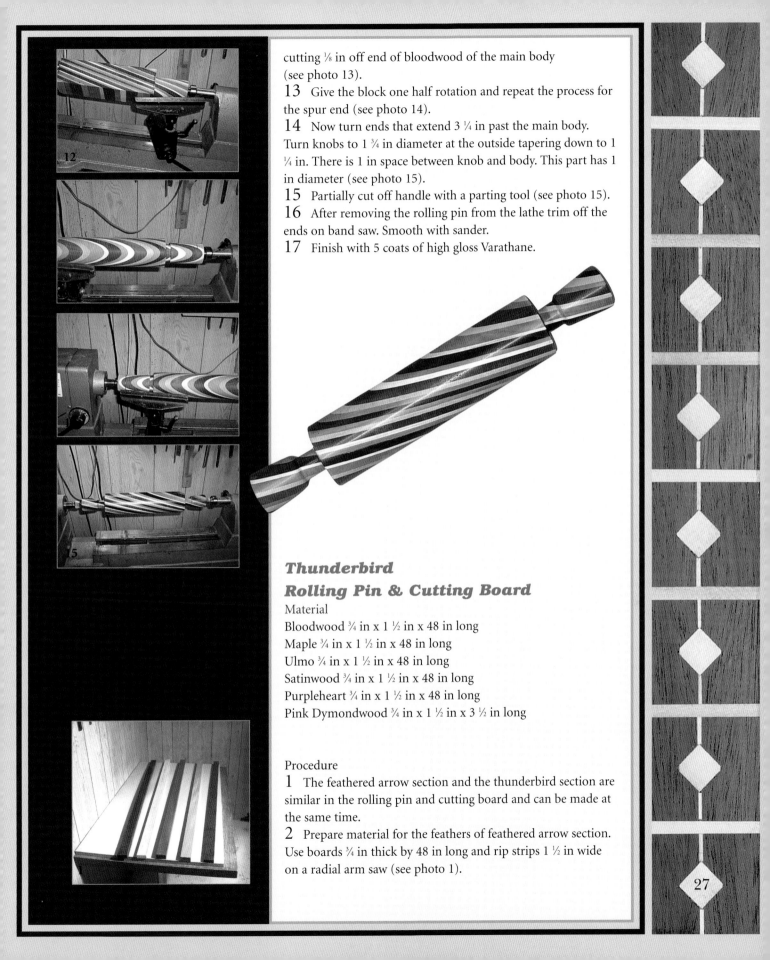

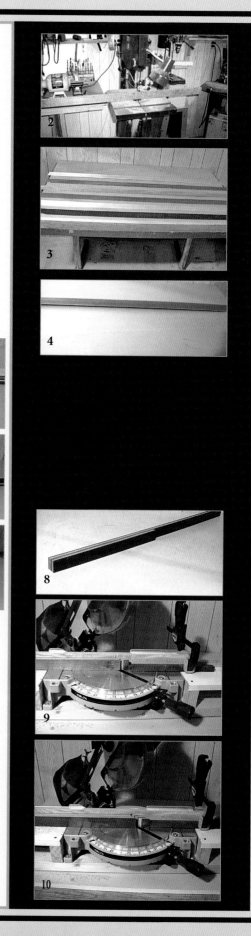

3   Split these strips on a band saw making them ¼ in thick (see photo 2).

4   Plane these down to ⅛ in thick on a thickness planer. This is as thin as I can safely go with the planer to produce one piece of bloodwood, 2 pieces of maple, 2 pieces of ulmo, 1 piece of satinwood, and 1 piece of purpleheart, each 48 in x 1 ½ in x ⅛ in (see photo 3).

5   For the feather, glue the maple to the bloodwood with yellow carpenter's glue. Allow to set for one hour. Plane the maple down to 1/16 in thick.

6   Glue the ulmo to the maple. When glue is set, plane it down to 1/16 in (see photo 4).

7   Glue the satinwood to the ulmo and plane down to 1/16 in. Then glue the second strip of ulmo to the satinwood and plane down to 1/16 in.

8   Glue second strip of maple to ulmo and plane to 1/16 in, giving ⅛ in bloodwood, 1/16 in maple, 1/16 in ulmo, 1/16 in satinwood, 1/16 in ulmo, 1/16 in maple. All woods are 48 in long (see photo 5).

9   To one end of this strip glue 32 in purpleheart ⅛ in thick (see photo 6). Cut off extra 16 in (see photo 7).

10   Tip over and glue the maple face to the purpleheart. It is easier to handle the material in the longer length; that is why I combine the 2 thicknesses as one piece (see photo 8).

11   Make 12 shorter pieces for the arrowhead and 12 longer pieces for the outer feathers. Set miter saw at 45° and use a stop block to cut 12 pieces ⅜ in long for shorter feathers. Cut 12 pieces ¾ in long for outer feathers (see photos 9, 10, 11, 12, 13, 14).

12   Cut 1 in pink Dymondwood at 45° for center of arrowhead (see photo 12). Glue shorter feathers to arrowhead and edge them with ⅛ in bloodwood (see photo 13). Glue shorter feathers to arrowhead and edge them with ⅛ in bloodwood. Three of these are needed (see photo 14).

13   For remainder of project use bloodwood and ulmo. Prepare material in 24 in lengths. All are 1 ½ in wide and ¾ in, ⅜ in, and ¼ in thick respectively. Run them across the jointer to shave off 1/32 in to leave a smooth edge (see photo 15).

14   Use ⅜ in piece of ulmo and cut into 12 pieces at 45° at both ends but in opposite directions. Make pieces 2 ¼ in long

28

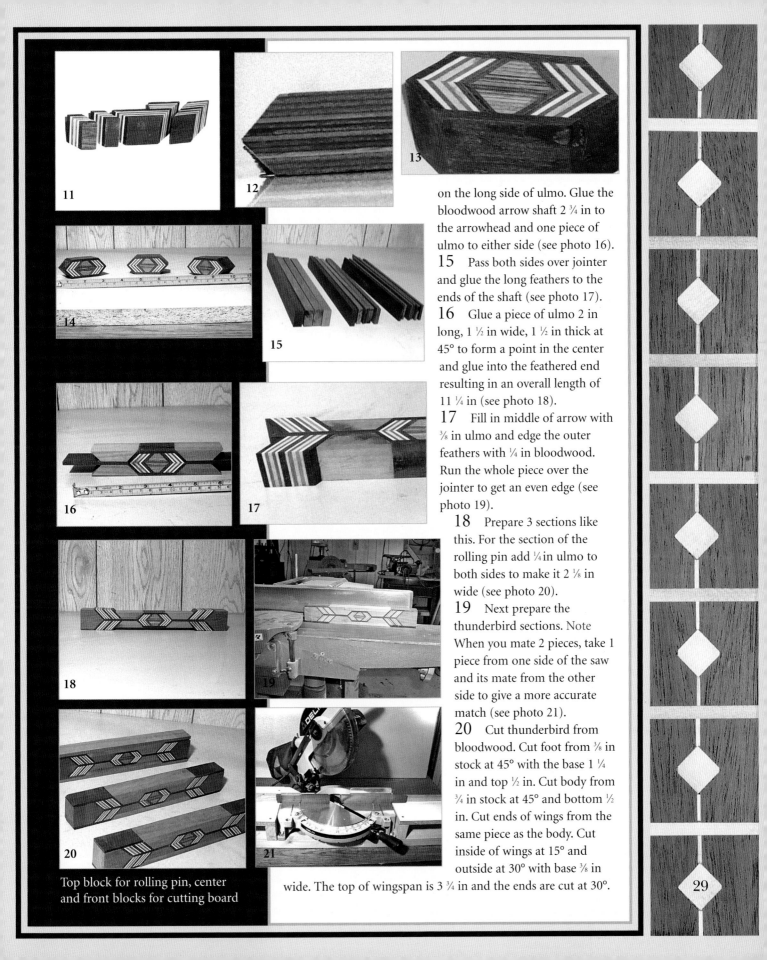

11

12

13

14

15

16

17

18

19

20

21

on the long side of ulmo. Glue the bloodwood arrow shaft 2 ¾ in to the arrowhead and one piece of ulmo to either side (see photo 16).

15 Pass both sides over jointer and glue the long feathers to the ends of the shaft (see photo 17).

16 Glue a piece of ulmo 2 in long, 1 ½ in wide, 1 ½ in thick at 45° to form a point in the center and glue into the feathered end resulting in an overall length of 11 ¼ in (see photo 18).

17 Fill in middle of arrow with ⅜ in ulmo and edge the outer feathers with ¼ in bloodwood. Run the whole piece over the jointer to get an even edge (see photo 19).

18 Prepare 3 sections like this. For the section of the rolling pin add ¼ in ulmo to both sides to make it 2 ⅛ in wide (see photo 20).

19 Next prepare the thunderbird sections. Note When you mate 2 pieces, take 1 piece from one side of the saw and its mate from the other side to give a more accurate match (see photo 21).

20 Cut thunderbird from bloodwood. Cut foot from ⅜ in stock at 45° with the base 1 ¼ in and top ½ in. Cut body from ¾ in stock at 45° and bottom ½ in. Cut ends of wings from the same piece as the body. Cut inside of wings at 15° and outside at 30° with base ⅜ in wide. The top of wingspan is 3 ¾ in and the ends are cut at 30°.

Top block for rolling pin, center and front blocks for cutting board

29

Cut neck from ⅜ in stock at 30°. Top of neck is ¾ in wide. Cut head from ¼ in stock. Cut back of head at 30°. Top is ¾ in long and cut beak at 45° (see photo 22).

21 Use ulmo 11 ¼ in long x ¼ in thick for thunderbird sections and glue the foot to the center. Fill in the ends with ⅜ in ulmo (see photo 23).

22 Set body on top of foot (see photo 24).

23 Place ¾ in ulmo cut at 45° at end to the body and at 15° to inside of the wing. Glue with yellow carpenter's glue. Place and glue the wing ends to this piece. Allow to dry one hour. Pass top over the jointer (see photo 25).

24 Trim the top of the wingspan flush with the outside of the wing ends. Glue into place and cut ¼ in ulmo at 30° and fill in the ends. On one end of the thunderbird section, the filler strip runs 3 in past the main body to allow for the handle. Allow to dry for one hour. Pass over the jointer (see photo 26).

25 Glue the neck and ends to body. Top is then jointed (see photo 27).

26 Glue head to neck and ends and joint. This completes the thunderbird. Glue ¼ in ulmo to the top of final section of the feathered arrow and one of the thunderbird section to split each in two for the rolling pin (see photo 28).

27 Mark one section of feathered arrow and one of thunderbird section to split each one in two for the rolling pin (see photo 29).

28 Cut along this marked line on the band saw. First for the thunderbird (see photo 30), then the feathered arrow section, (see photo 31).

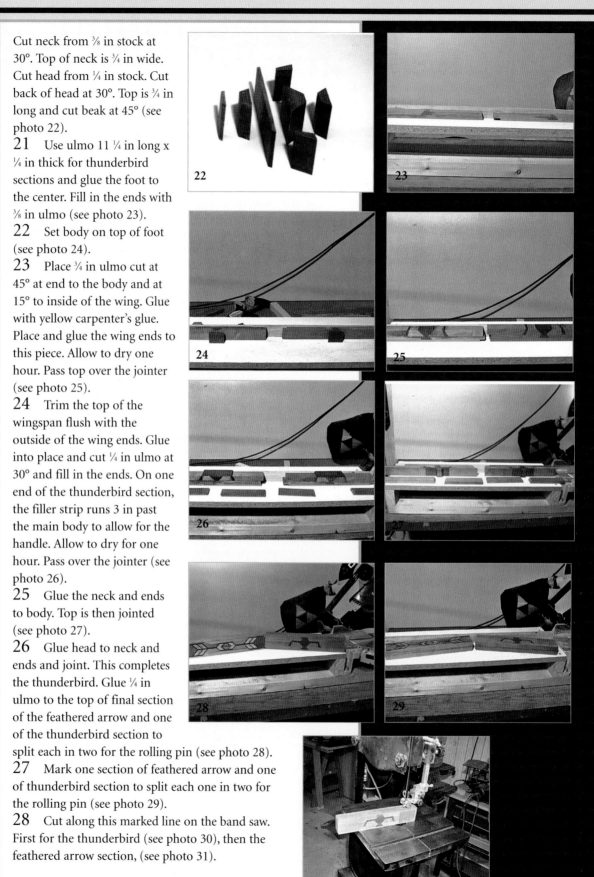

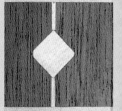
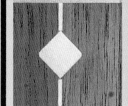

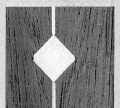

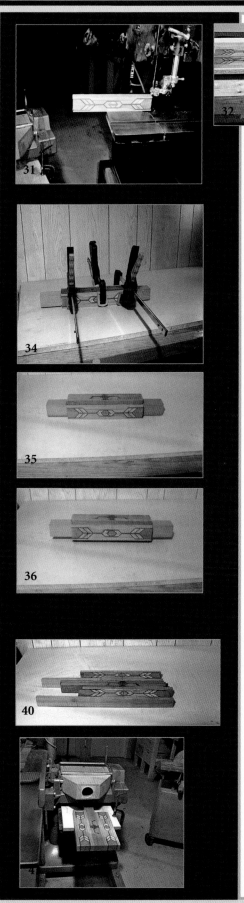

32

33

31

34

35

36

40

29 Now 4 faces for the rolling pin are prepared (see photo 32).

30 Use pieces of 18 in ulmo 1 ⅞ in square and glue piece of bloodwood ⅛ in x 2 in wide to 4 sides to produce a 2 ⅛ in square (see photo 33).

31 To opposite sides glue one of the sections of the split arrow sections of 31 (see photo 34).

32 Glue one of the split thunderbird sections to one side of the rolling pin (see photo 35).

33 Glue the other half to the alternate side (see photo 36).

34 To mount this part on the lathe, use calipers to mark the ends for the center point and the spur. Be accurate (see photo 37).

37

35 Design emerges as it is turned on the lathe. Cut the main body back to 11 in x 3 in diameter. Knob is turned to 1 ¾ in on the outside. Connecting link is 1 in long x 1 in diameter. The link and knobs are 3 in length (see photo 38). Finish with 3 coats of high gloss Varathane.

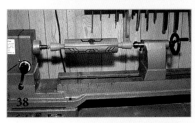

38

36 For cutting board glue one arrow section to thunderbird section with ¾ in ulmo spacer in between and ¾ in border on the outside (see photo 39). Allow to set (see photo 40).

39

37 Trim off excess from board and use thickness planer on both sides to get 1 ⅛ in thick (see photo 41).

38 Shape handle to match rolling pin knobs. Round the edges with the router (see photo 42).

39 Finish same as rolling pin.

42

Thunderbird Bowl

Material

Mahogany	1 ½ in x 10 in x10 in
Mahogany	3 ½ in wide
Maple	3 ½ in wide
Wenge	3 ½ in wide
Walnut	3 ½ in wide
Pau amarillo	3 ½ in wide

Make 2 blocks for each design
Bowl is 12 in diameter and 4 ½ in high (see photo 1)

Procedure

1   Cut pieces for thunderbird from walnut (see photo 2).
Legs Use ½ in walnut cut at 45°; reverse piece and cut again with narrow part ½ in for top of legs (see photo 3)
Body Use ¾ in walnut cut at 45°; bottom is ½ in wide
Wing tip Use ¾ in walnut cut at 33° for the outside and 15° for inside which is ¼ in wide at top (see photo 4).
Wingspan Use ³⁄₁₆ in walnut cut at 33°; length at top is 3 ½ in. (see photo 6).
Neck Use ½ in walnut cut at 33°; top of neck is ½ in wide (see photo 5).
Head Use ³⁄₁₆ in walnut cut at 33° and beak at 45°; top is 1 in long. All cut pieces form thunderbird (see photo 7).

2   From ½ in pau amarillo cut 2 filler strips at 45° to match the leg for each thunderbird block (see photo 8).

3   To a 6 in piece of pau amarillo glue a leg in the center and a filler strip on both sides (see photo 9). Allow to dry for one hour. NOTE When gluing up wider material there is always some variation in the glue line. The thickness given for pieces is slightly more than needed so you can pass each layer over the jointer to true it up as you proceed (see photo 10).

4   Add body and wing tips to legs with appropriate filler strips of pau amarillo. True up the top (see photo 11).

5   Add wingspans and filler strips and true up (see photo 12).

6   Finish thunderbird by gluing neck and head and a final layer of ³⁄₁₆ in pau amarillo (see photo 13).

7 For the serrated design of the blocks use ⁵⁄₁₆ in walnut and pau amarillo and 3 ½ in wide wenge for the accent block (see photo 14).

8 Plane 3 ½ in wide wenge down to ¼ in thick. From this board at 45° angle cut 4 pieces that are ½ in long on the short side. Glue the 2 short sides together to form a block (see photo 15)

9 Edge all sides with maple veneer to show an accent line (see photo 16)

10 Cut these pieces for the serrated walnut block: 4 pieces 3 ½ in long by ⁵⁄₁₆ in thick angled in the same direction, 2 pieces 3 ½ in long angled in the opposite direction, 2 pieces 2 ½ in long angled in the opposite direction (photo 17).

11 All the boards are now ⁵⁄₁₆ in thick and 3 ½ in wide. In the center of a 12 in piece of pau amarillo glue a 2 ½ in piece of walnut and fill in the ends. Allow glue to cure for one hour and true up the top before adding the 3 ½ in walnut piece and filling in the ends (see photo 18).

12 Add the accent block made up previously (see photo 19). Add 2 pieces of 2 ¼ in walnut to each end of the accent center and fill the ends with pau amarillo (see photo 20).

13 Top off the block to match the bottom part. Pare down all 4 blocks to 2 in thick and 3 ¼ in wide, the thunderbird blocks 5 ¾ in long, and the serrated block 12 in long (see photo 21)

14 Material is now ready to assemble for the lathe. Glue 10 in x 10 in x 1 ½ in block of mahogany to faceplate. I turn it to 10 in diameter (see photo 22).

15 Plane wenge to ¹⁄₈ in thickness. After gluing a layer of maple veneer to mahogany, laminate a width of wenge to the maple, extending 1 in all around past the outside (see photo 23).

33

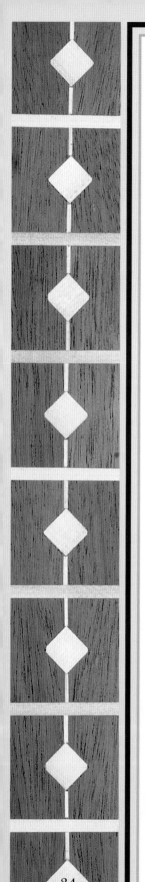

24

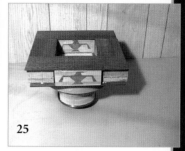
25

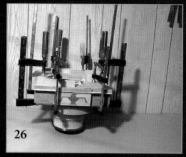
26

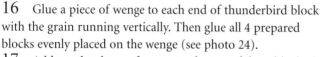

16 Glue a piece of wenge to each end of thunderbird block with the grain running vertically. Then glue all 4 prepared blocks evenly placed on the wenge (see photo 24).

17 Add another layer of wenge to the top of these blocks (see photo 25).

18 Top off wenge with a layer of ¾ in mahogany. Use sufficient clamps to make sure all glued surfaces make contact (see photo 26).

19 The block is now ready for turning. Cut away all the excess to make the bowl (see photo 27). Excavate inside of bowl (see photo 28)

20 Give bowl a coat of wood filler before parting it off the faceplate. While it is still on the lathe it makes it much easier to rub in the filler and aggressively sand it (see photo 29). Finish the same as rolling pin.

27

28

29

Wine Cooler Stand

Material
Bubinga 1 in x 12 in x 30 in and 2 in x 2 in x 21 in
Plywood 1 piece ¾ in thick (see photo 1)
Screws 4

Procedure

1 Attach plywood to faceplate with 4 screws (see photo 2). Turn plywood to 8 in diameter. On the lathe index at 45°.

2 At 7 in diameter drill 8 holes at the index line and attach ¾ in bubinga to plywood with 1 ¼ in screws (screw holes in bubinga will become holes for spindles of basket (see photo 2).

3 With parting tool cut out the middle of bubinga leaving ⅞ in ring. Shape inside and outside of ring (see photo 3).

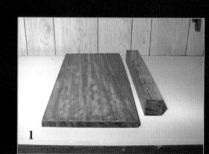
1

2

3

34

4 The spacer on the faceplate has 1 in pin. Drill 1 in hole on a piece of bubinga that was cut into 7 in circle (see photo 4).

5 Slide these two together and with a block on the live center put pressure on the bubinga and shape it (see photo 5).

6 Top ring is ⅞ in by 8 in diameter. Base is 6 ¼ in with 1 in hole that is ½ in deep on the bottom of the base (see photo 6).

7 Use 8 pieces ¾ in x ¾ in x 6 in length (see photo 7). Turn to the desired shape with ½ in ends (see photo 8).

8 Center of holes on top ring are ½ in from outside and form 7 in circle. Center of holes in base are ½ in outside and form 5 in circle. The distance between the top and the base is 5 in. Square shows that the spindles need to be at an 11° angle (see photo 9).

9 Set the table on drill press at 11°. Clamp jig to table of drill press and drill ½ in hole ½ in deep at previously indexed hole on top of ring (see photo 10). Reverse jig on the drill press and drill holes in the base .

10 Top ring, 8 spindles, base, and assembled basket are now complete (see photos 11 & 12).

11 Draw design for 3 feet and cut on the band saw (see photos 13 & 14).

12 Round off 2 in x 2 in for the pedestal. Finish only the lower part that will be mortised for the feet (see photo 15). On the lathe mark the bottom of the pedestal at 120° for the three feet.

13 Cut a mortise ⅜ in with a chisel before finishing the pedestal (see photo 16).

14 Make final cut on the feet (see photo 17).

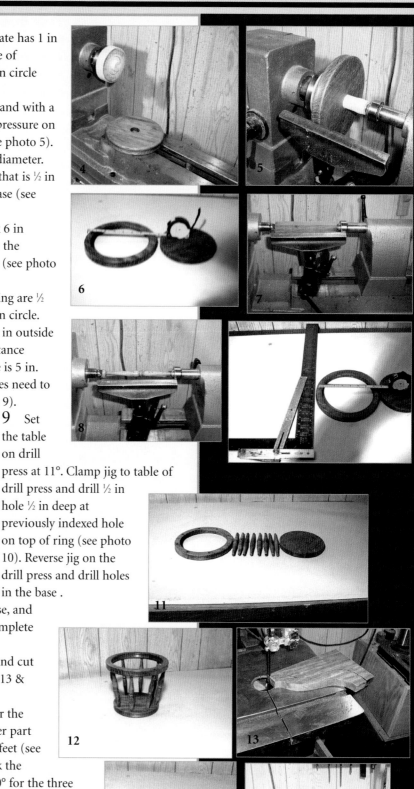

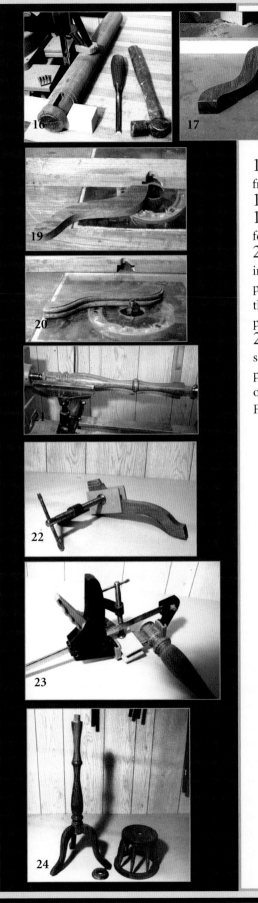

15 With the router cut the tenons on the feet (see photo 18).

16 Cut both sides of feet to leave $\frac{3}{8}$ in tenon (see photo 19).

17 With a rounding bit on the router, detail the top of the feet from both sides (see photo 20).

18 Finish the detail on the pedestal (see photo 21).

19 To provide a straight edge, clamp 2 pieces of board to the foot (see photo 22).

20 Glue the tenon of the foot into the mortise on the pedestal and apply pressure to the glued-up joint (see photo 23).

22 Turn a small collar to give some reinforcing to top of pedestal where it enters the base of the basket (see photo 24). Finish with high gloss Varathane.

37

Winged Chess Bowl

Material

Bubinga   2 in x 10 in x 24 in (see photo 1)

Procedure

1   Trim wood piece to 8 in x 24 in. Use piece cut off for knob and pillars. Cut 8 in x 24 in piece in 3 pieces 8 in x 8 in. Use 1 for base, 1 for bowl, 1 for lid.

2   Reinforce edges of piece for bowl with 2 in x 2 in wood to prevent tearout when turning (see photo 2).

3   To have access to the top and bottom of the bowl for turning, fasten 4 in block to the first faceplate of lathe for surface to support the bowl (see photo 3).

4   First faceplate has 4 holes 2 ½ in apart. With 5 in screws attach the bowl block to the 4 in spacer and faceplate. Screw holes will become holes for the pillars (see photo 4).

5   Turn inside of bowl to 5 ½ in center. Corners of bowl are raised up (see photo 5).

6   Shape bottom of bowl from the other side (see photo 6).

7   Glue second bubinga block for base to the block fastened to second faceplate. Piece can then be shaped as you wish (see photo 7).

8   Glue 8 in x 8 in piece for the lid to a spacer on the third faceplate. Hollow out the bottom of the lid (see photo 8).

9   Begin shaping top of lid from the outside (see photo 9).

10   Use a small block on the live center to support the lid as you work toward the middle (see photo 10). Make ½ in hole in center of top of lid for the knob. Turn ½ in pin, ½ in long on the spacer. Fit into the hole on lid top. Turn the top of the lid toward this pin (see photo 10).

38

1

2

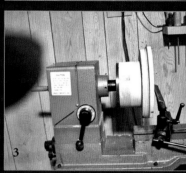

5

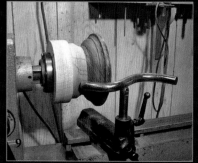

6

7

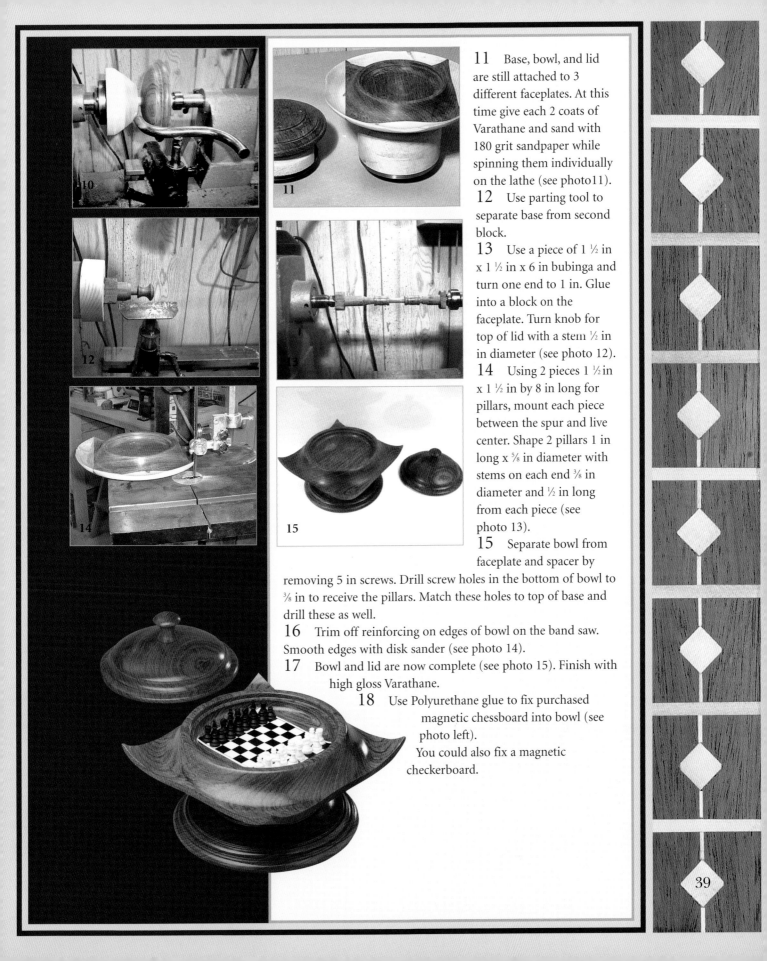

11 Base, bowl, and lid are still attached to 3 different faceplates. At this time give each 2 coats of Varathane and sand with 180 grit sandpaper while spinning them individually on the lathe (see photo11).

12 Use parting tool to separate base from second block.

13 Use a piece of 1 ½ in x 1 ½ in x 6 in bubinga and turn one end to 1 in. Glue into a block on the faceplate. Turn knob for top of lid with a stem ½ in in diameter (see photo 12).

14 Using 2 pieces 1 ½ in x 1 ½ in by 8 in long for pillars, mount each piece between the spur and live center. Shape 2 pillars 1 in long x ⅝ in diameter with stems on each end ⅜ in diameter and ½ in long from each piece (see photo 13).

15 Separate bowl from faceplate and spacer by removing 5 in screws. Drill screw holes in the bottom of bowl to ⅜ in to receive the pillars. Match these holes to top of base and drill these as well.

16 Trim off reinforcing on edges of bowl on the band saw. Smooth edges with disk sander (see photo 14).

17 Bowl and lid are now complete (see photo 15). Finish with high gloss Varathane.

18 Use Polyurethane glue to fix purchased magnetic chessboard into bowl (see photo left).

You could also fix a magnetic checkerboard.

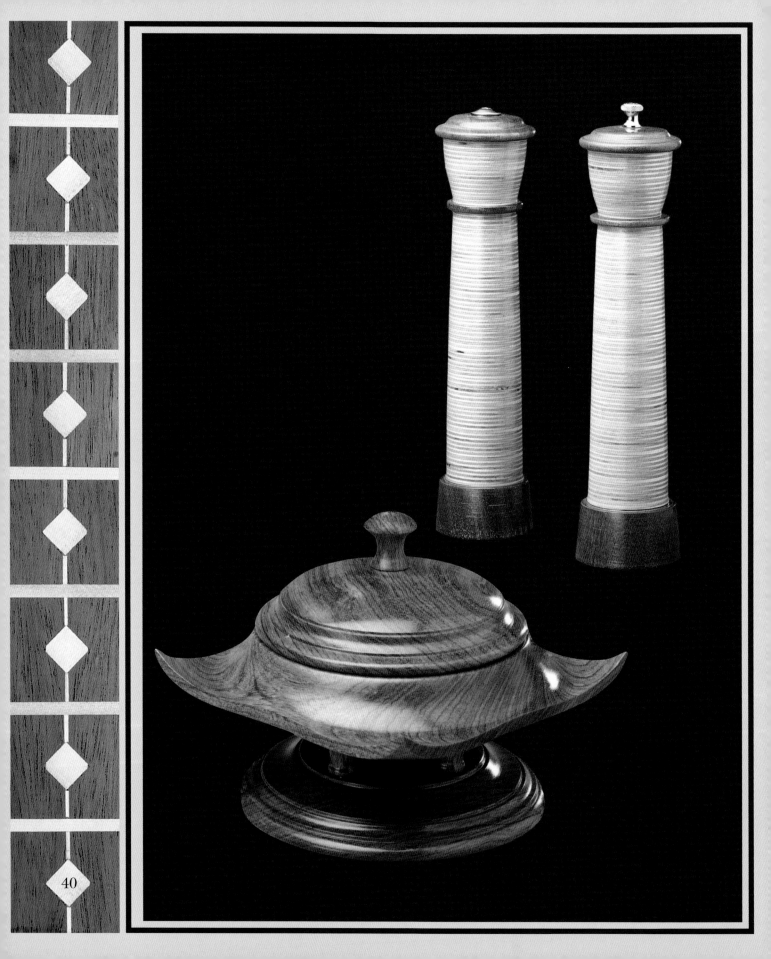

Lighthouse Salt & Pepper

Material
Philippine mahogany 4 in x 6 in x 6 in long
Baltic birch plywood 24mm thick and 24 in x 48 in.

Procedure

1 Use mahogany material for base, middle accent line, and top. Cut Baltic birch into 3 in strips. Glue 3 of these together (see photo 1).

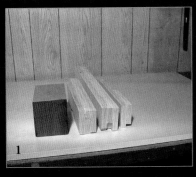

2 Cut strips into nine 3-in squares (see photo 2).

3 Use calipers to mark center of squares (see photo 3).

4 Use 3/4 in bit to drill hole through each center (see photo 4).

5 Use purchased mechanism for salt and peppermill. Cut center shaft to desired length (see photo 5).

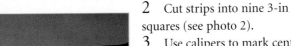

6 For base of the peppermill use 1 ½ in of 3 in x 3 in piece of mahogany. Drill the bottom with a 1 ¾ in bit ½ in deep. Drill remainder with 1 ⅛ in bit (see photo 6).

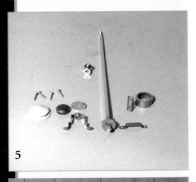

7 Peppermill has this base, plus 3 of the triple layered blocks, 1 single layer of plywood, 1 in x 3 in x 3 in mahogany, on 2-layered plywood block, and ½ in of mahogany for the top (see photo 7). Single layer of 3 in x 3 in plywood has ⅞ in hole in the center.

8 Glue triple layered blocks and single layer plywood for the bottom of the mill. Glue 1 in mahogany and double layer of plywood, and ½ in mahogany top together and drill in the center with ¼ in bit (see photo 8).

9 Bottom for the peppermill is now ready (see photo 9).

10 Glue top and bottom of peppermill. Assemble salt in same way, accent piece in

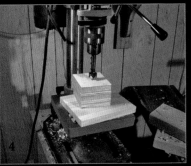

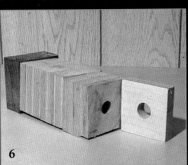

41

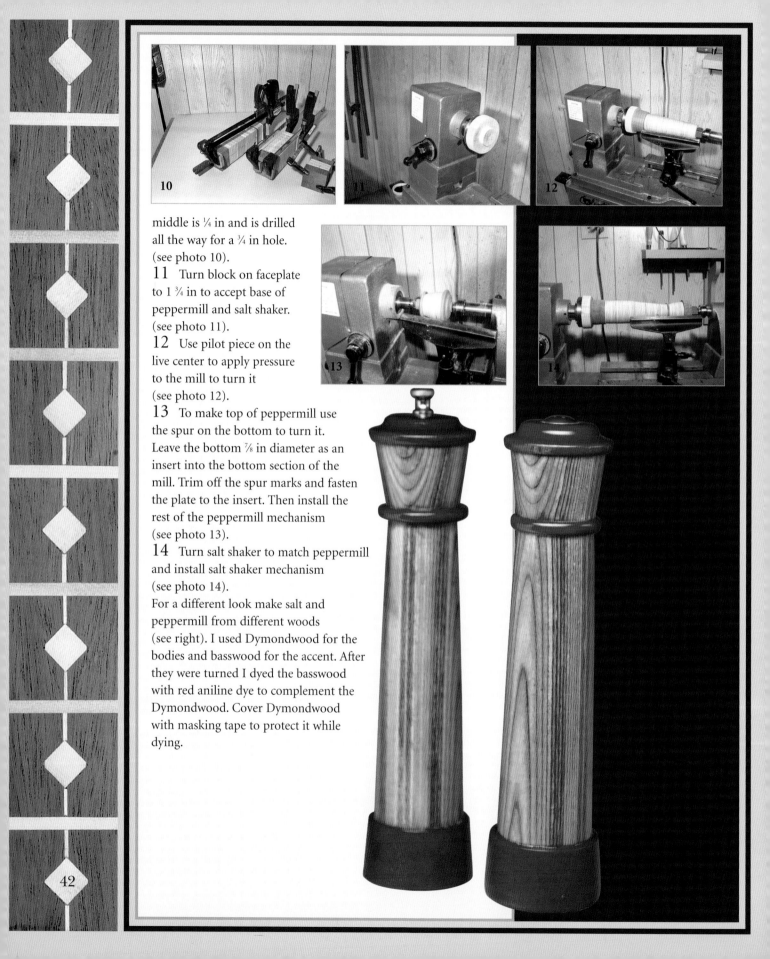

middle is ¼ in and is drilled all the way for a ¾ in hole. (see photo 10).

11 Turn block on faceplate to 1 ¾ in to accept base of peppermill and salt shaker. (see photo 11).

12 Use pilot piece on the live center to apply pressure to the mill to turn it (see photo 12).

13 To make top of peppermill use the spur on the bottom to turn it. Leave the bottom ⅞ in diameter as an insert into the bottom section of the mill. Trim off the spur marks and fasten the plate to the insert. Then install the rest of the peppermill mechanism (see photo 13).

14 Turn salt shaker to match peppermill and install salt shaker mechanism (see photo 14).

For a different look make salt and peppermill from different woods (see right). I used Dymondwood for the bodies and basswood for the accent. After they were turned I dyed the basswood with red aniline dye to complement the Dymondwood. Cover Dymondwood with masking tape to protect it while dying.

Turned Objects from Man-made Materials

Perfume Applicator turned from a one to one epoxy mixing ratio
Pen and pencil set turned from Dymondwood
Man's pen turned from Dymondwood
Lady's pen turned from Dymondwood — Tim Bergen

Small bowl turned from 2 to 1 mixing ratio epoxy and alabaster — Tim Bergen

Large bowl turned from Parallum beam material — John Hiebert

Harm Hazeu

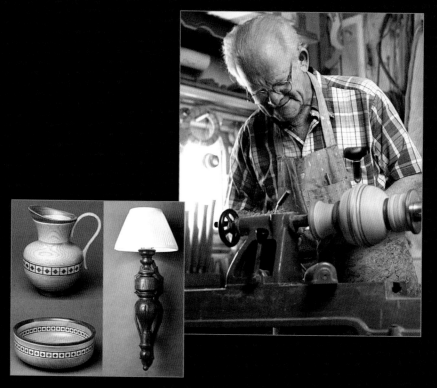

I was born in Pynacker, The Netherlands, and went to school there until I was 12 years old. Then I worked full time in the market gardens and later with a carpenter in a small shop. That was a turning point for me. The carpenter owned a lathe and introduced me to woodturning. I started with small boxes and other small items that were easy to turn as I learned the basic skills of the craft. I had to leave that job because it was too dangerous in the city during the Second World War. After the war I worked for another shop that made turned wood wall and table lamps and I stayed until I emigrated to Canada in 1956. I got a job in Winnipeg with a company that made custom furniture and soon I was doing all the wood turning for the company. I worked there for 29 years and I made hundreds of furniture items and experimented with some intricate and unusual turning.

When I retired I added a small workshop to my house and I continue to pursue woodtuning. It is an activity that I have loved all my life. I still make lamp bases and fancy chair rungs, but my interests have broadened to more complicated scroll work and laminated wood patterns. I enjoy working with exotic woods to make decorative vases and bowls. I decide what I want to make and work out the pattern beforehand. The designs are as simple or as complicated as I want to make them. Sometimes I work a rare wood into the pattern. It is interesting to me to experiment with the pairing of different woods and textures to get the effects I want.

I have a medium heavy lathe and a minimum of tools which have turned out to be my favorites over the years. Every woodworker finds the most comfortable tools for the work he does. I enter my work at woodworking shows and enjoy making special pieces for gifts for family and friends.

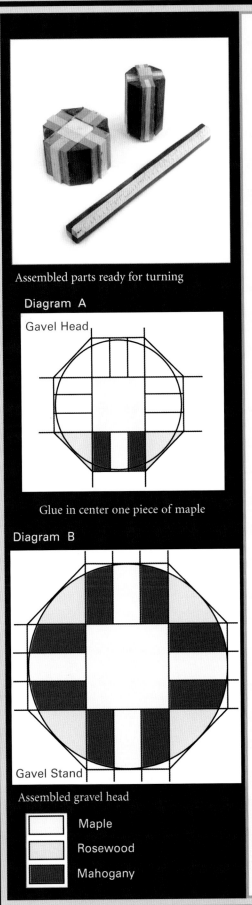

Assembled parts ready for turning

Diagram A

Gavel Head

Glue in center one piece of maple

Diagram B

Gavel Stand

Assembled gravel head

- ☐ Maple
- ☐ Rosewood
- ■ Mahogany

Gavel and Stand

Material

Maple 1 piece each

  20 in x ⅞ in x ⅜ in, 12 in x 1 ¼ in x ¾ in,
  6 in x ⅞ in x ⅞ in, 3 in x 2 in x 2 in
  12 in x 1 ⅛ in x ½ in

Mahogany 2 pieces each

  20 in x ⅞ in x ¼ in, 12 in x 1 ¼ in x ⅝ in,

Rosewood 1 piece each

  10 in x 1 in x 1 in, 6 in x 1 ⅜ in x 1 ⅜ in,
  12 in x 1 ⅛ in x ½ in

Procedure

Gavel Head

1   Glue 1 piece of maple 20 in x ⅞ in x ⅜ in between 2 pieces of mahogany, 20 in x ⅞ in x ¼ in. Cut in four (pieces are 5 in long). Glue on piece of maple 6 in x ⅞ in x ⅞ in. Use white or yellow wood glue. See diagrams A for assembled gavel head.

2   Cut a piece of rosewood 10 in x 1 in x 1 in on the diagonal lengthwise (see illustration 1) for the gavel. Cut these pieces in two lengthwise and glue in the corners.

3   Place gavel head on lathe between centers and turn to dimensions shown in diagram C, p46.

Stand

4   Cut a piece of rosewood 6 in x 1 ⅜ in x 1 ⅜ in on the diagonal lengthwise. Cut these pieces in two and glue in the corners. Glue 1 piece of maple 12 in x 1 ¼ in x ¾ in between 2 pieces of mahogany 12 in x 1 ¼ in x ⅝ in. Cut in 4 (pieces are 3 in long) and glue on a piece of maple 3 in x 2 in x 2 in. See diagram B to assemble stand.

5   Sand stand on one side and screw to faceplate of lathe and turn to dimensions shown on diagram D, p46.

Handle

6   Glue 1 piece of maple 12 in x 1 ⅛ in x ½ in to one piece of rosewood 12 in x 1 ⅛ in x ½ in. Allow to dry. Cut in two pieces and glue as shown in illustration 2.

7   Turn on lathe according to diagram E, p46.

8   Drill hole in gavel head and glue in handle.

9   Finish with 4 or 5 coats of Varathane semi gloss professional finish.

Illustration 1

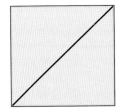

Cut rosewood on diagonal

Illustration 2

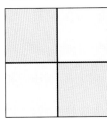

To make handle, glue maple & rosewood. Cut in two and glue

45

Diagrams show dimensions for turning gavel head, stand, and handle
Scale - half size

Diagram C

$^1/_2$ in

$^5/_{16}$ in

2 $^1/_8$ in

$^5/_{16}$ in
$^1/_2$ in

2 $^3/_6$ in

Diagram D

2 $^3/_4$ in

$^3/_4$ in

1 in

$^3/_4$ in

4 in

Diagram E

1 in

$^5/_{16}$ in

9$^1/_8$ in

1 in

1$^7/_8$ in

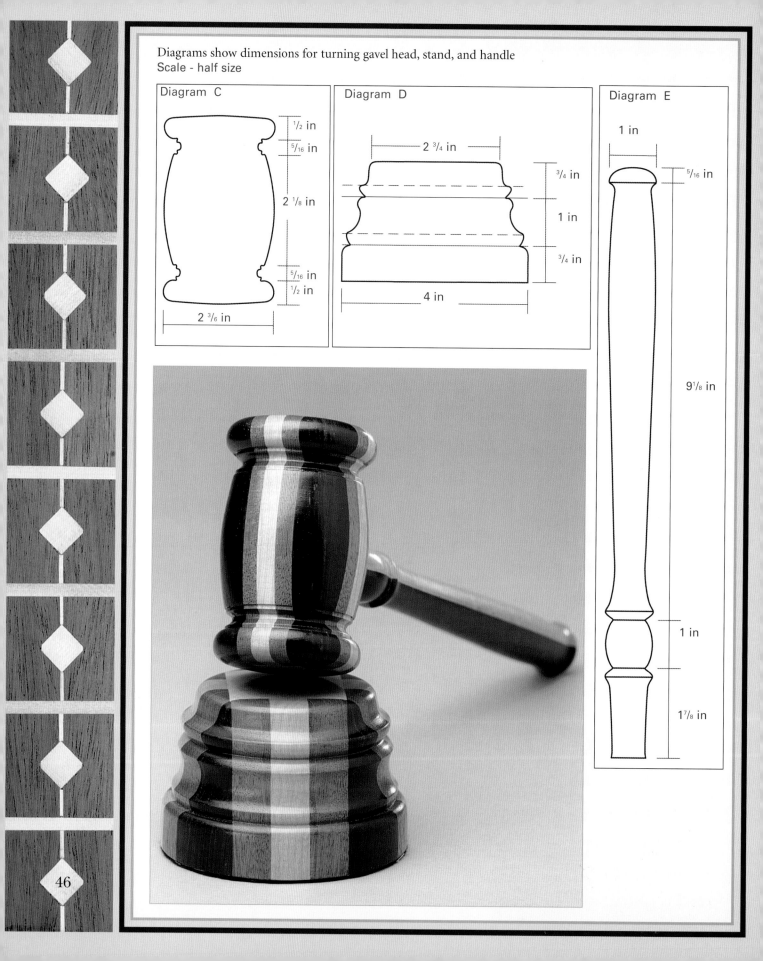

Scroll Work Plate

Material
Walnut 7 in diameter round piece x 1 in thick
Maple 36 in x 3 in x ¾ in

Procedure

1   Screw walnut to faceplate and turn a tenon in it. Use specifications for one-way chuck with correct # jaws for size of base of plate.

2   Cut maple into 6 segments with 30° angle as shown in diagram. Glue together in circle and use band clamp. Set aside to dry.

3   With the chuck on the lathe put on walnut and round it. True up the front.

4   Sand or plane the maple on one side and glue to walnut, making sure it is exactly centered (see photo at left).

5   Turn it to start at back and then front, according to diagram A, p48. Sand with 100 to 120 grit sandpaper and finish with 220 grit sandpaper.

6   Transfer rim pattern (use clear velum to trace design and use carbon paper to transfer to rim of plate) so all of rim has the pattern.

7   Drill small hole for scroll saw and cut out each design.

8   Sand and finish with 4 or 5 coats of Varathane semi gloss professional finish.

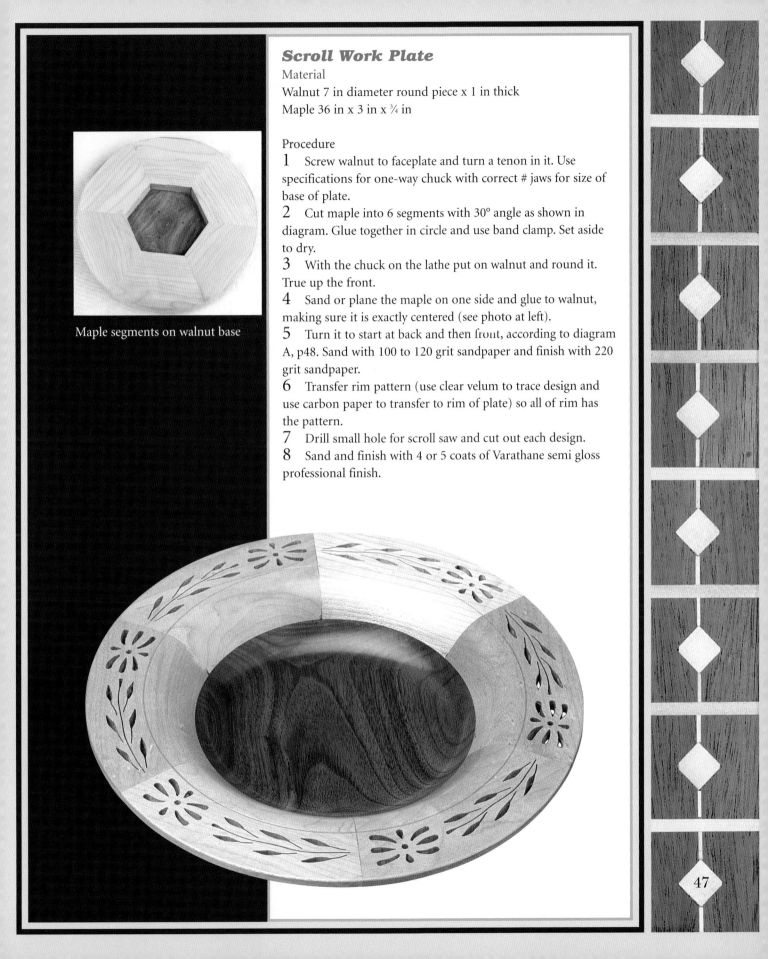

Maple segments on walnut base

Diagram A Scroll Work Plate
Scale - half size

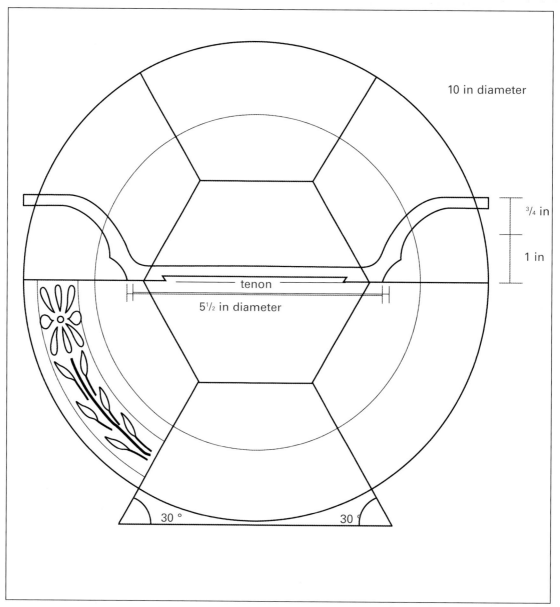

10 in diameter

3/4 in

1 in

tenon

5 1/2 in diameter

30 °   30 °

Scroll Work Rim Pattern
Scale - full size

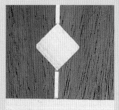
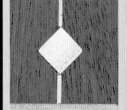

Patterned Vase

Material

Body

Ash	5 ½ in round x 2 in thick	2 pieces
Ash	3 ½ in round x ½ in thick	1 piece
Ash	3 ½ in round x 2 in thick	1 piece
Walnut	3 ½ in round x ½ in thick	2 pieces
Cherry	4 in round x ½ in thick	1 piece
Mahogany	26 in x 1 in x ⅛ in thick	2 strips
White Birch	26 in x 1 in x ⅛ in thick	2 strips
Walnut	24 in x 2 in x ¾ in thick	1 piece
Sepalia	26 in x 1 in x ³⁄₁₆ in thick	1 piece
Maple	30 in x 2 in x ³⁄₁₆ in thick	2 pieces

Handles

Ash	5 ½ in x 4 in x ³⁄₁₆ in thick	2 pieces
Mahogany	4 in x 5 ½ in x ⅛ in thick	1 piece

Procedure

1   Screw 3 ½ in scrap wood 1 in thick to faceplate of lathe. True front and glue 3 ½ in ash x ½ in thick to it. True front again and glue 3 ½ in walnut ½ in thick to it. Glue on 1 piece ash 5 ½ in round x 2 in thick. True front and cut it round.

2   Cut 4 pieces of walnut 24 in x 2 in x ¾ in as shown on pattern at left. Sand both sides and cut off ⅛ in with band saw on both sides. Sand again and repeat until you have 16 pieces. Fit 4 pieces and glue on the ash with the smooth side down. Turn on lathe to ¹⁄₁₆ in and cut the outside round with chisel.

3   Glue 2 strips of mahogany to 2 strips of white birch. Plane the edge and cut with table saw down to ¾ in wide.

4   Set the cross fence at ± 4° and screw on strip of scrap wood same thickness. Use another small strip to nail down as a stop so you can cut off ⅜ in pieces, as shown in diagram A at left.

5   For the first rim you need 44 pieces (see photo 1). It is easier to glue two together, one with birch up and one with mahogany up. Glue together and place on paper to dry. Place elastic around the ash. Then put the 44 pieces on the walnut (see photo 2). Clamp in 4 places and put elastic around it to make sure it holds tightly. Take off 3

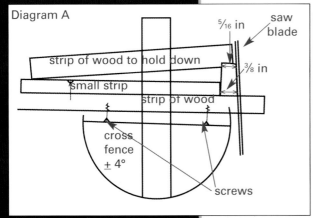

elastic band

1

Pattern for walnut pieces

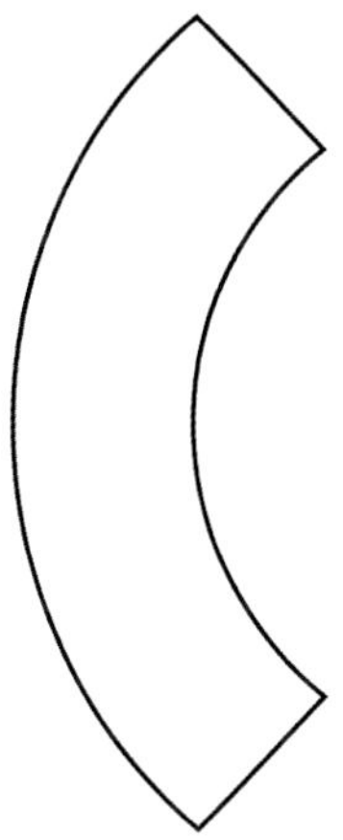

Scale - half size

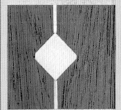

Diagram A

⁵⁄₁₆ in saw blade

strip of wood to hold down

⅜ in

small strip

strip of wood

cross fence ± 4°

screws

Diagram A top view

center of bowl

rim of bowl

⁵⁄₁₆ in

⅜ in

³⁄₁₆ in overlap

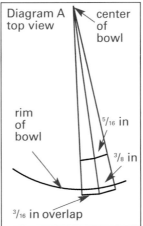

49

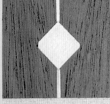

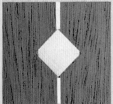

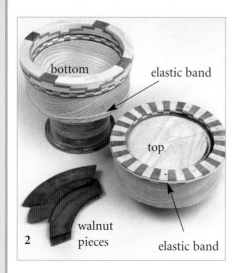

bottom · elastic band · top · walnut pieces · elastic band

2

clamps and make sure all joints are closed. If not sand to fit. Glue on this rim and true around outside. Then fit and glue on 4 pieces of walnut. Let dry. Trim again to ¹⁄₁₆ in.

6   For the next 4 layers, cut 24 pieces from sepalia as shown in diagram B. For the first layer place 4 pieces with same distance between and fill in with maple. Turn down to ⅛ in thick. Next layer put on two pieces of sepalia just overlapping the first one, as shown in diagram C and fill in with maple. Shaded area is sepalia the rest is all maple. Turn down to ⅛ in thick. Repeat until the last piece overlaps, as shown in diagram. This should be ¼ in larger than the last rim. (see photo 3)

Diagram C

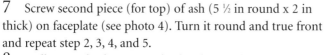

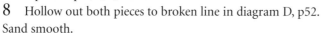

7   Screw second piece (for top) of ash (5 ½ in round x 2 in thick) on faceplate (see photo 4). Turn it round and true front and repeat step 2, 3, 4, and 5.

8   Hollow out both pieces to broken line in diagram D, p52. Sand smooth.

9   Finish the inside with Varathane professional finish. Allow to dry. Then glue together making sure it is exactly centered (see photos 4 and 5). Take off the top faceplate and turn the outside, as shown in diagram. True front and glue on walnut piece 3 ½ in round x ½ in thick. True again and cut through to the inside.

5

10   Drill 1¼ in hole from bottom of ash piece 3 ½ in round x 2 in. Glue piece on top of walnut. Round and true the top. Glue on the cherry piece 4 in round x ½ in. Finish turning the outside and hollow out the top, as shown in diagram D, p52. Sand all with 100 grit sandpaper, then 20 grit and 220 grit.

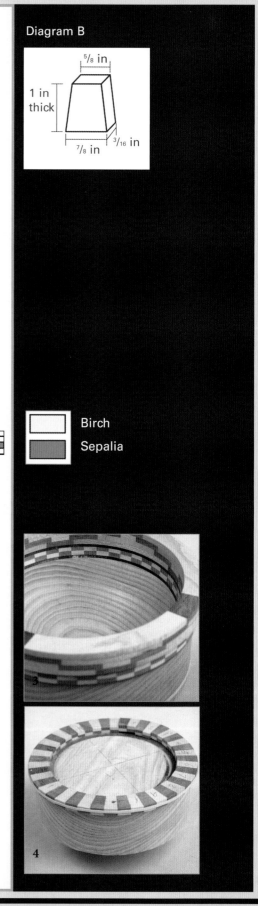

Diagram B

5/8 in
1 in thick
7/8 in
3/16 in

Birch
Sepalia

3

4

50

11 To make handles, glue a piece of mahogany 4 in x 6 in x ⅛ in between two pieces of ash 6 in x 4 in x ³⁄₁₆ in so that the grain of mahogany is running across from the ash. See patter p52.

12 Cut handles apart as shown by dotted lines. Fit the two parts that will be glued to the vase. Then cut out on pattern lines. Sand and round the edges.

13 Finish the vase and handles with 4 or 5 coats of Varathane professional finish before gluing on the handles. Then sand the spots where the handles will be glued to vase. Glue on handles. Hold with elastic until dry.

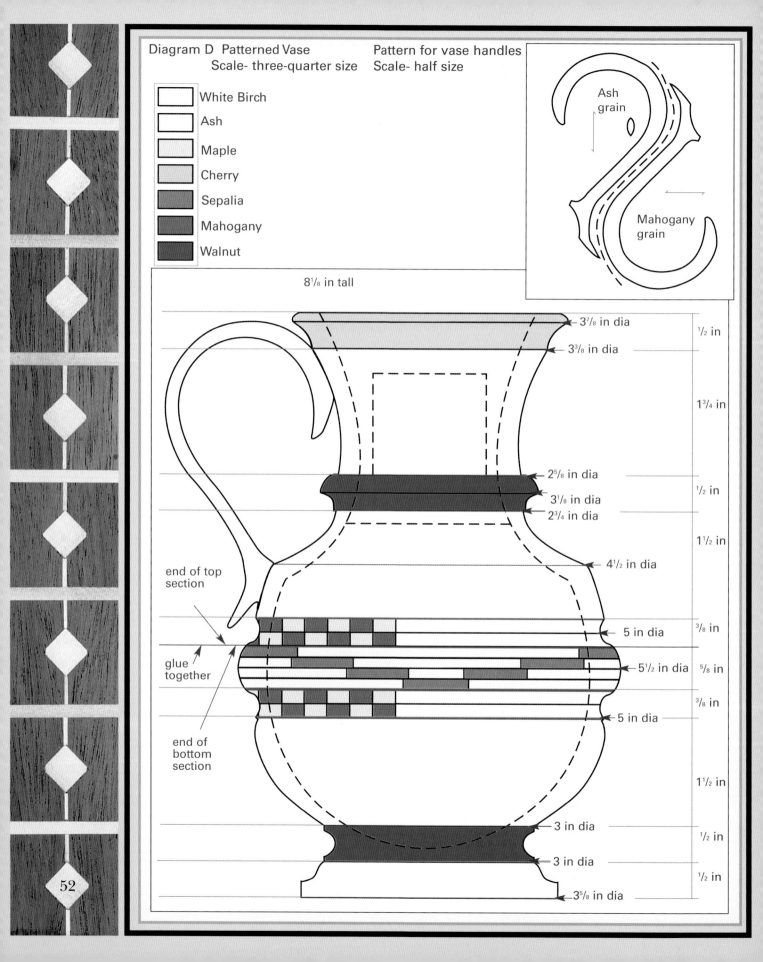

Diagram D Patterned Vase
Scale- three-quarter size

Pattern for vase handles
Scale- half size

Ash grain

Mahogany grain

- ☐ White Birch
- ☐ Ash
- ☐ Maple
- ☐ Cherry
- ☐ Sepalia
- ☐ Mahogany
- ☐ Walnut

8$^1/_8$ in tall

3$^7/_8$ in dia — $^1/_2$ in

3$^3/_8$ in dia

1$^3/_4$ in

2$^5/_8$ in dia — $^1/_2$ in

3$^1/_8$ in dia

2$^3/_4$ in dia

1$^1/_2$ in

4$^1/_2$ in dia

end of top section

glue together

end of bottom section

5 in dia — $^3/_8$ in

5$^1/_2$ in dia — $^5/_8$ in

5 in dia — $^3/_8$ in

1$^1/_2$ in

3 in dia — $^1/_2$ in

3 in dia — $^1/_2$ in

3$^5/_8$ in dia

52

Walnut Bowl

Material

Walnut	8 in x 8 in x 2 in	1 piece
Rosewood	30 in x 1 in x ⅝ in	1 piece
Sepalia	26 in x 2 in x ¾ in	1 piece
Elm	26 in x 2 in x ¾ in	1 piece
Elm	26 in x 1 in x ¾ in	1 piece

1 Screw walnut to faceplate and cut 8 in circle on band saw. True up the face and turn a tenon and foot, as shown in diagram A. For tenon use chuck specifications. Take walnut off faceplate and put on chuck.

2 Cut with parting tool, as shown in diagram A, and take off top ring which is used later. With ring removed cut out center pieces as shown in diagram A.

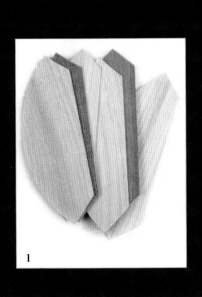

1

Diagram A

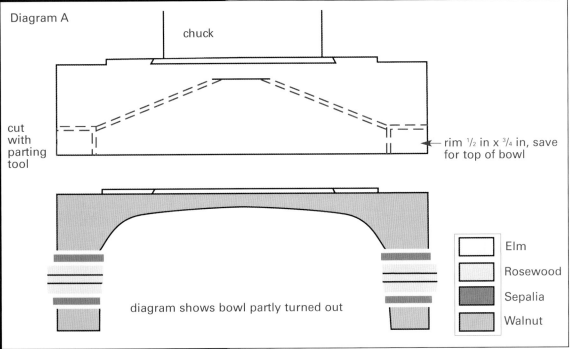

chuck

cut with parting tool

rim ½ in x ¾ in, save for top of bowl

diagram shows bowl partly turned out

☐	Elm
☐	Rosewood
☐	Sepalia
☐	Walnut

2

3 From 26 in x 2 in x ¾ in elm, cut 4 pieces as shown in pattern on p55. Sand both sides and cut ⅛ in off on both sides on band saw. Sand again and repeat until you have 16 pieces. Do the same with sepalia but cut ¼ in thick until you have 8 pieces.

4 True edge of bowl and fit 4 elm pieces (see photo 1) with the smooth side down and glue. True face again on lathe. Repeat with sepalia and repeat again with elm.

5 Drill ¼ in holes 1 in apart in the center of the rosewood piece 30 in x 1 in x ⅝ in on the ⅝ in side (see photo 2). On the table saw put the cross fence at 7° with strip of wood screwed on the cross fence, as shown in diagram B. On a small strip of

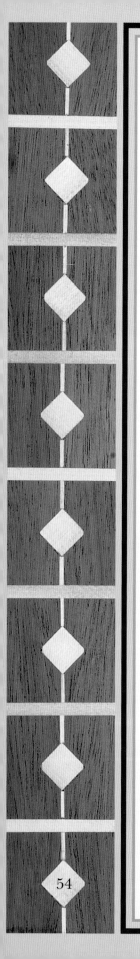

wood drill ¼ in hole, as in rosewood, and put in a dowel so that the rosewood fits on it (see diagram B). Nail the small strip to cross fence so that you can cut the rosewood pieces to measurements given in diagram B top view. Note Always try first with scrap wood.

6   Cut strips of elm 1 in x ⅛ in. Cross cut them to put between rosewood. Glue one to each piece of rosewood. Place elastic around the walnut base. Place rosewood on the rim of the bowl without glue (see photo 4). Clamp in 4 places. Slip the elastic around rosewood. Take 3 clamps off and see if all joints are closed. If not, sand to fit. Glue down. This rim should be ¼ in larger than the walnut. On the lathe true the rosewood rim on face and side. Repeat step 4 with elm, sepalia, and again with elm. Then glue on walnut ring that you had cut off.

7   With ¼ in plug cutter, cut out a white birch plug and glue one in each hole in rosewood.

8   Turn the inside and outside according to diagram dimensions. Sand carefully with 100 or 120 grit and finish with 220 grit.

9   Finish with 4 or 5 coats of Varathane professional finish semi gloss.

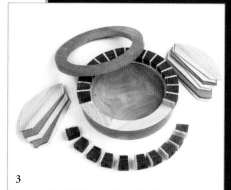

3

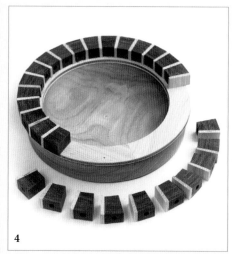

4

Diagram B

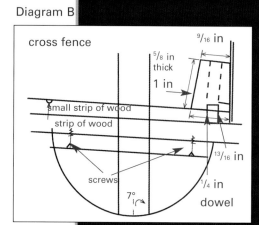

cross fence

⁹⁄₁₆ in

⁵⁄₈ in thick

1 in

small strip of wood

strip of wood

¹³⁄₁₆ in

screws

7°

¼ in

dowel

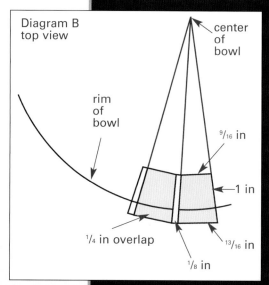

Diagram B top view

center of bowl

rim of bowl

⁹⁄₁₆ in

1 in

¼ in overlap

¹³⁄₁₆ in

⅛ in

Pattern Walnut Bowl
Scale - half size

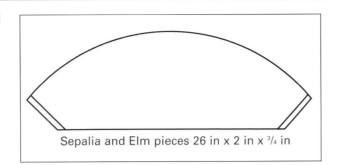

Sepalia and Elm pieces 26 in x 2 in x ¾ in

Diagram C   Side view of bowl

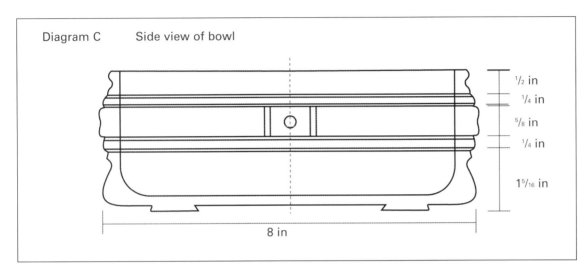

$\frac{1}{2}$ in

$\frac{1}{4}$ in

$\frac{5}{8}$ in

$\frac{1}{4}$ in

$1\frac{5}{16}$ in

8 in

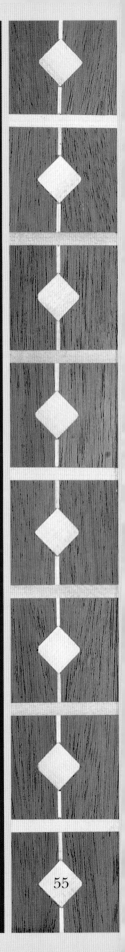

55

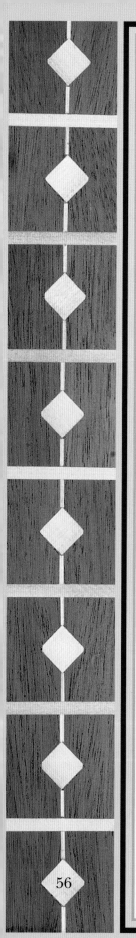

Keepsake Box with Lid

Material

Cherry wood	8 in x 8 in x 2 in	1
Honduras mahogany	8 in x 6 in x 1⅛ in	1
Walnut	12 in x 2 in x 1 in	1
Basswood	12 in x 2 in x 1 in	2
White birch	small amount	

Veneers of oak, Spanish mahogany, walnut, birch

Procedure

1 Begin by resawing cherry, one piece ¾ in thick and one piece 1⅛ in thick. Cut 8 in circle on both. Screw 1⅛ in piece on faceplate and cut in a tenon, using chuck specifications. Remove from faceplate and put on chuck. Turn round and true front.

2 From basswood cut three ⅛ in strips and from remainder of basswood and walnut cut 2 pieces from each as shown in pattern right. Sand both sides and cut off ⅛ in on both sides. Repeat until you have 8 pieces each of walnut and basswood.

3 Fit 4 pieces of walnut to the cherry and glue with the smooth side down. This should be ¼ in larger than the cherry. Round and true face on the lathe. Repeat with basswood.

4 From mahogany cut across the grain 6 pieces 1⅛ in. Put a groove bit with 90° angle in table-mounted router and cut grooves, as shown in diagram (A). Then cut little squares from white birch across the grain to fit in the grooves. Use birch veneer between, as shown in diagram (B). Glue together as a strip.

5 Cut strip in 1 in pieces by setting the cross fence at ± 7° angle (see diagram C, p57) to cut these pieces with the little squares in the center.

6 From the basswood strips ⅛ in x 1 in cut pieces the height of the blocks to put between them and glue one to each piece (see photos 1). Put elastic around the cherry wood and put the mahogany pieces on the rim and clamp down on four places. Slip elastic around it (see photo 2) and check if all joints are closed. If not, sand to fit. This rim can be glued down again. It should be ¼ in larger than the cherry. Round and true the front.

7 Repeat step 2 but begin with the basswood first and then the walnut.

8 Put ⅛ in layer of cherry on top. Box is ready to

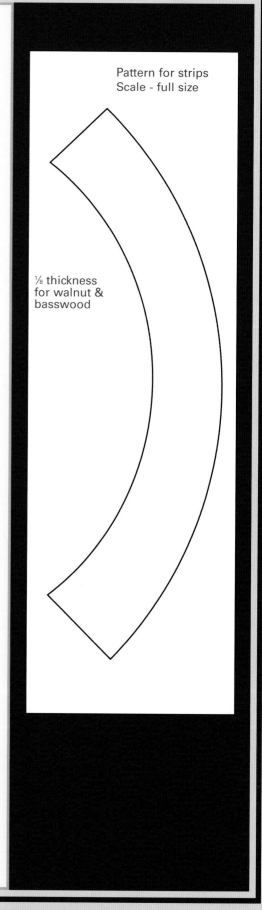

Pattern for strips
Scale - full size

⅛ thickness for walnut & basswood

Diagram A Cut grove

Diagram B

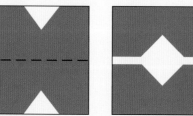

| | White birch |
| | Mahogany |

Cut on broken line and glue diamond patterns together with a small veneer piece of birch

Diagram C

cross fence

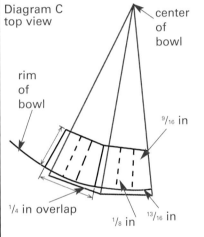

small strip of wood

strip of wood

screws

5/8 in thick

1 in →

9/16 in

13/16 in

1/4 in dowel

7°

Diagram C top view

center of bowl

rim of bowl

9/16 in

13/16 in

1/4 in overlap

1/8 in

turn inside and outside, as shown in diagram (D).

9 Make the inlay for the cover first. Photocopy the pattern twice (half cover face p 58) to get the full circle or draw it on paper. Cut the veneer, as shown in diagram E, and glue to the paper with paper glue. Then cut a circle ± 7 in.

10 Put ¾ in cherry on faceplate using small screws that don't penetrate the wood more than ¼ in. Turn the inside. Put a piece of plywood on faceplate and true the face and turn it to fit the inside of the cover. Hold to plywood with 2-way tape.

11 Then turn in ¹⁄₁₆ in of the circle of the veneer. Glue in veneer with the paper up and place corrugated cardboard on top and then plywood. Clamp down.

12 When dry sand and scrape off the paper and finish turning. Then turn knob and glue.

13 Sand everything carefully using 100 or 120 grit and then 220 grit.

14 Finish with 4 or 5 coats of Varathane professional finish semi gloss.

1

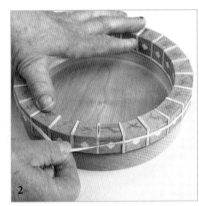

2

Pattern Keepsake Box - Scale - half size

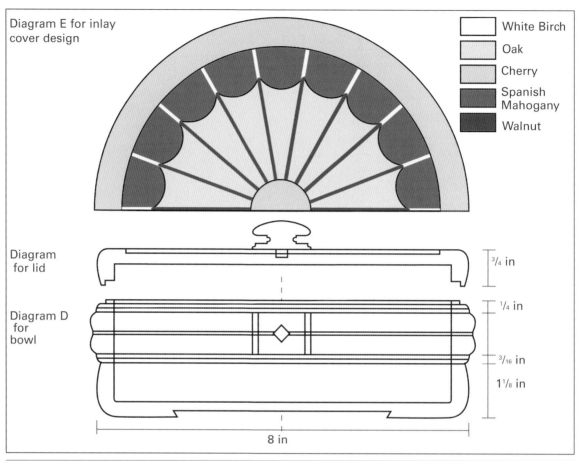

Diagram E for inlay cover design

	White Birch
	Oak
	Cherry
	Spanish Mahogany
	Walnut

Diagram for lid

Diagram D for bowl

3/4 in

1/4 in

3/16 in

1 1/8 in

8 in

Applewood Candlestick

Material
Applewood 2 ¼ in x 2 ¼ in x 8 ¾ in long
Applewood 5 in x 5 in x 1 in thick

Procedure

1   Drill hole ⅝ in diameter and ½ in deep in end of applewood piece 2 ¼ in x 2 ¼ in x 8 ¾ in. Turn plug that fits in hole, as shown in pattern.

2   Turn to dimensions provided in pattern.

3   For base, screw wood on faceplate and turn tenon according to chuck specifications. Place on chuck and turn to dimensions given in pattern. Sand.

4   Finish with 4 or 5 coats of Varathane professional finish semi gloss.

5   You can use other woods for this candlestick (see photo below which is ebony and white birch).

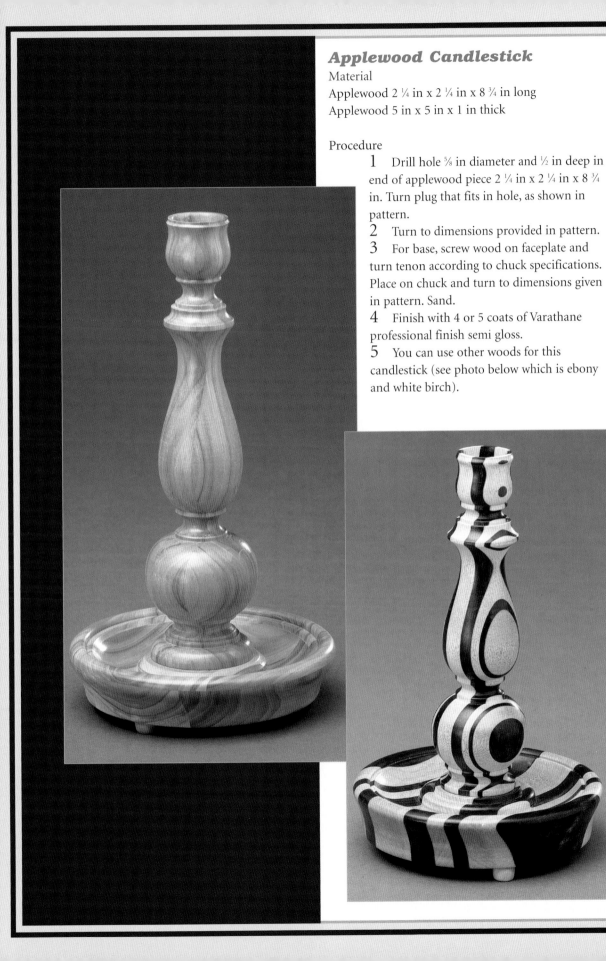

59

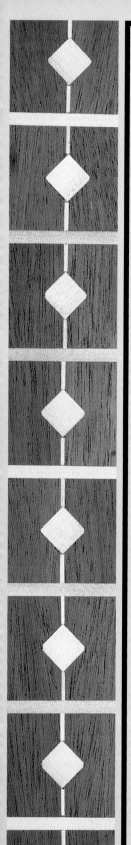

Diagram Applewood Candlestick
Scale - three quarter size

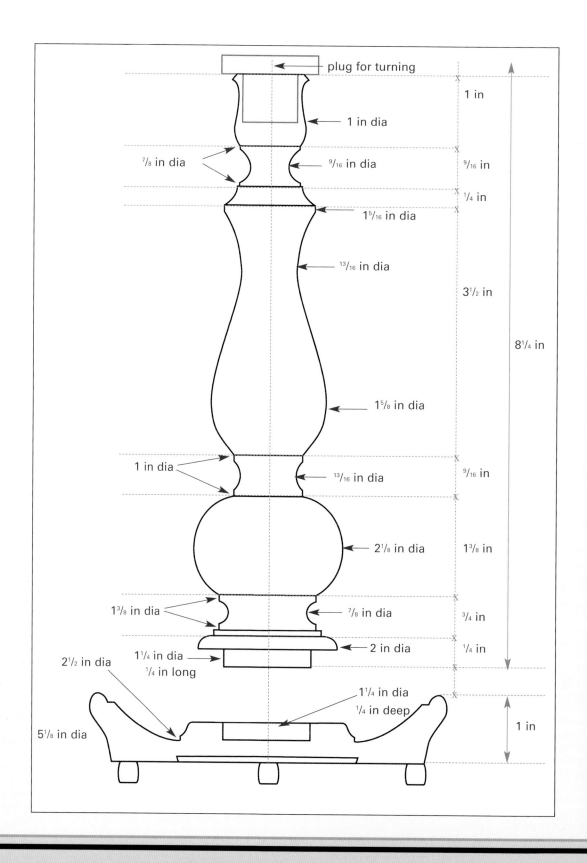

plug for turning

1 in

1 in dia

⁷/₈ in dia

⁹/₁₆ in dia

⁹/₁₆ in

¹/₄ in

1⁵/₁₆ in dia

¹³/₁₆ in dia

3¹/₂ in

8¹/₄ in

1⁵/₈ in dia

1 in dia

¹³/₁₆ in dia

⁹/₁₆ in

2¹/₈ in dia

1³/₈ in

1³/₈ in dia

⁷/₈ in dia

³/₄ in

2 in dia

¹/₄ in

1¹/₄ in dia
¹/₄ in long

2¹/₂ in dia

1¹/₄ in dia
¹/₄ in deep

5¹/₈ in dia

1 in

60

Tim Bergen

I have always been interested in woodworking. My first opportunity to work with quality tools and lumber was in shop classes in school and during summer holidays when I worked for my uncle as a carpenter's helper. I studied architecture too and drew projects that I could build from wood. For twenty years I built houses and apartments and made and installed kitchen cabinets and oak crown moldings. Later I worked for a company doing concrete restoration, a physically demanding job which permanently injured my knee and now prevents me from doing construction work.

During my recovery from knee surgery my youngest daughter came into my workshop and asked me to make her a wood pen and that's how my woodturning began, I made pens for family and friends and they became more fancy and intricate as I experimented with different woods and the effects of laminating them together. I enjoyed it so much I found it difficult to leave my workshop. When I added bowls and vases as projects my excitement with woodturning became almost obsessive. The challenge of cutting and gluing different woods to make an elaborate design was very rewarding. Soon I was assembling hundreds of pieces to make the designs I created myself. Usually I figure out the pattern on my computer before I begin and then it's a matter of being very careful and exact with cutting the pieces to realize the object. For me, woodturning has become an art form that allows me to create intricate patterns to make beautiful objects. It is rewarding to cut and glue all the pieces together and watch the object and design take shape.

My designs are quite time consuming to produce and I have included diagrams and step-by-step directions for making some fairly intricate pieces. The pen projects are easier to make but allow for creative input in the choice of woods and wood scraps to be laminated. The designs can be simple or complex and can incorporate as many different woods as you need. I have found that straight-grained hardwoods work the best for these sets. Choose the combinations you like the best. I am fascinated with woodturning and I experiment with different materials and new methods every day. Like other turners I take my work to woodworking shows, but now I have so many requests for my pieces that I take orders and am in my workshop all hours, day and night.

Pen and Pencil Sets

Materials

Bloodwood ¾ in x ¾ in x 5 in
African blackwood ¾ in x ¾ in x 5 in
(photo 1)

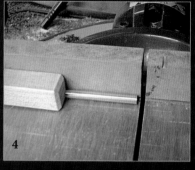
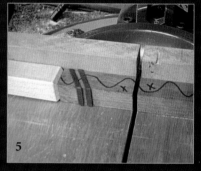
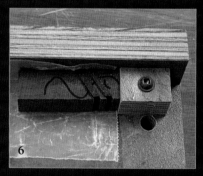
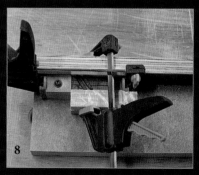

Procedure

1   Set the chop saw 30° and a stop block to get ¹⁄₁₆ in piece for the strips (photo 2) – 4 for each pen (don't raise blade until it has stopped or blade catches small piece and throws it).

2   Leave saw set at 30° and set up for cutting the blanks. Make a mark ¹⁄₁₆ in from end of the bloodwood blank (which will be tip of pen). Align mark with saw kerf on right side of blade and cut off the wedge-shape piece (see photo 3). Note   Lines are marked along one side of pen blank so pieces can be put together in same order as cut.

3   Cut off ¹⁄₁₆ in piece from bloodwood as you did with the African blackwood. Set aside without mixing up the order of pieces. Use stop block and clamp to set up pen tube (see photo 4). Cut the blank ¹⁄₁₆ in longer than the tube and sand it flush later. Note   Measure from tooth of blade and not the blade itself so blank will not be too short.

4   Once you have proper dimensions clamp stop block in place and move brass tube out of the way and replace with the wood pieces. Line them up (see photo 5) using 2 African blackwood strips.

5   Cut off bottom part of pen and leave pieces in place. Mark an x on either side of the cut to ensure rematching of grain when pieces are put together (see photo 5).

6   From same end, cut the top off following same steps. Pieces are ready for gluing (see photo 6). Note   I made a simple gluing jig from scrap wood. Put wax paper under the pieces so they won't stick to the jig. I use polyurethane glue for exotic woods. Allow to dry for 5 – 12 hrs. Follow manufacturer's instructions. Apply glue to one of the mating surfaces and wet the other surface with water. Align markings. When all pieces are glued (see photo 7) a block of wood keeps the pieces tight up against the jig.

62

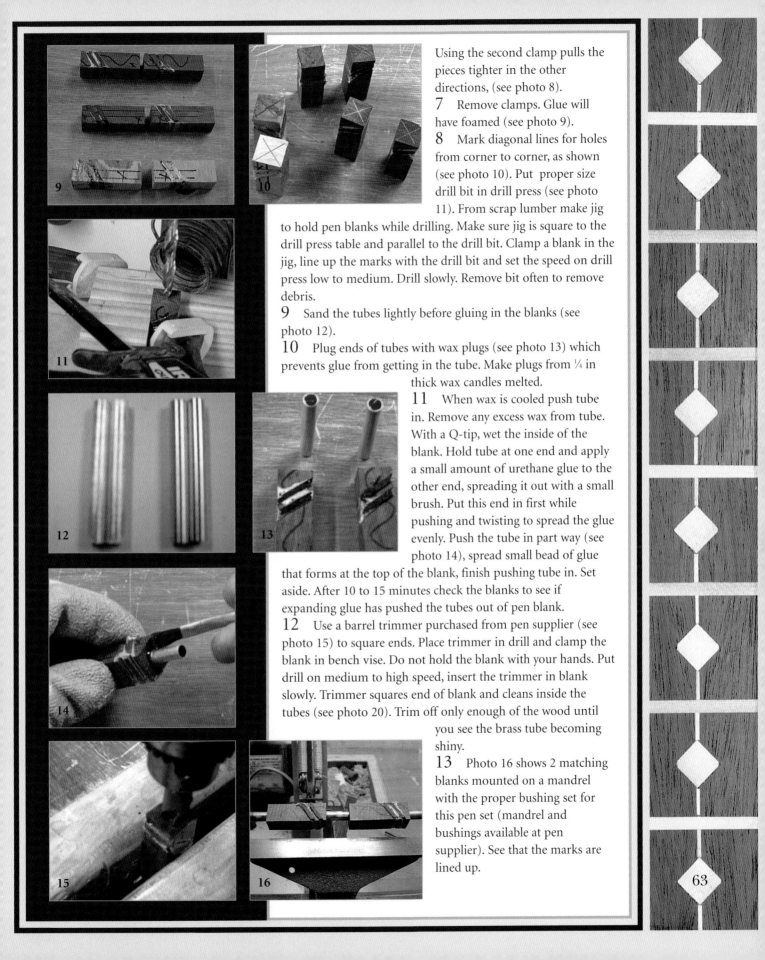

Using the second clamp pulls the pieces tighter in the other directions, (see photo 8).

7   Remove clamps. Glue will have foamed (see photo 9).

8   Mark diagonal lines for holes from corner to corner, as shown (see photo 10). Put proper size drill bit in drill press (see photo 11). From scrap lumber make jig to hold pen blanks while drilling. Make sure jig is square to the drill press table and parallel to the drill bit. Clamp a blank in the jig, line up the marks with the drill bit and set the speed on drill press low to medium. Drill slowly. Remove bit often to remove debris.

9   Sand the tubes lightly before gluing in the blanks (see photo 12).

10   Plug ends of tubes with wax plugs (see photo 13) which prevents glue from getting in the tube. Make plugs from ¼ in thick wax candles melted.

11   When wax is cooled push tube in. Remove any excess wax from tube. With a Q-tip, wet the inside of the blank. Hold tube at one end and apply a small amount of urethane glue to the other end, spreading it out with a small brush. Put this end in first while pushing and twisting to spread the glue evenly. Push the tube in part way (see photo 14), spread small bead of glue that forms at the top of the blank, finish pushing tube in. Set aside. After 10 to 15 minutes check the blanks to see if expanding glue has pushed the tubes out of pen blank.

12   Use a barrel trimmer purchased from pen supplier (see photo 15) to square ends. Place trimmer in drill and clamp the blank in bench vise. Do not hold the blank with your hands. Put drill on medium to high speed, insert the trimmer in blank slowly. Trimmer squares end of blank and cleans inside the tubes (see photo 20). Trim off only enough of the wood until you see the brass tube becoming shiny.

13   Photo 16 shows 2 matching blanks mounted on a mandrel with the proper bushing set for this pen set (mandrel and bushings available at pen supplier). See that the marks are lined up.

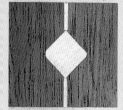

14   When blanks are set up on the lathe the tip of the pen is always towards the tail stock.

15   When the blanks are on the lathe and in the right order tighten the thumb screw finger tight (too tight causes the mandrel to bend and pen will be out of round. Turn the blanks on lathe (speed between medium-high and high) and use ¼ in spindle gouge. Set tool rest as close as possible and set height about center. Start cutting at an edge and work towards the center of the blank. For the top of the pen (the blank closest to the headstock) turn it down to the diameter of the bushings leaving ¹⁄₃₂ in for sanding. On the bottom, turn the blank to ½ in diameter, then from the tip of the pen measure in ³⁄₁₆ in from this point while the lathe is running (see photo 17), and use the gouge to taper down

to the bushing towards the tip (see photo 18). From this same mark towards the center of the pen make a ⅛ in cove (don't go too deep to expose the brass tube).

16   Taper remaining part of the upper portion of the lower blank towards the center bushing (see photo 18). With the lathe at its lowest speed start sanding with 180 grit sandpaper. Use a light touch and move back and forth quickly. Work your way up through grits to 300 grit. Stop the lathe periodically to check pen surface.

17   To finish pens I use lacquer-based Turner's polish which is easy to use and dries quickly with a high sheen and hard finish. Use a lint free cloth and apply a small amount of the finish thinned 50% with lacquer thinner. With the lathe running at medium to low speed

begin moving the cloth back and forth (see photo 19). Do not stop in any one spot. Keep the cloth moving until it becomes dry then apply a bit more pressure which creates friction and then the shine will start to appear. Apply as many coats as you wish. Follow the instructions for drying times.

18   I use plastic containers to organize all the small pieces for pen and pencil kits (see photo 20).

19   Assemble jig (see photo 21) from a piece of ¾ in material and 2 in carriage bolts which are drilled and epoxied in

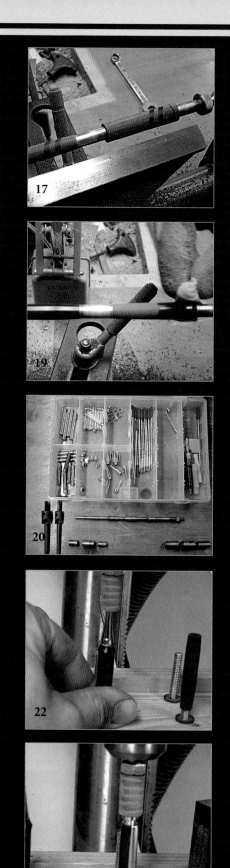

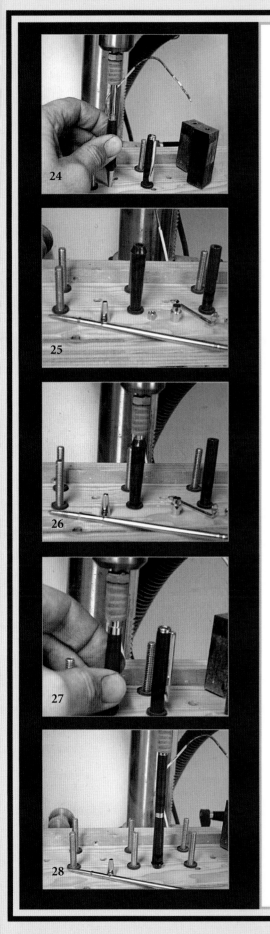

24

25

26

27

28

countersunk holes on the bottom so jig will sit flat. Put a small rubber washer on top to protect the pens. Photo 21 shows all the parts for pen on the drill press which also makes a great pen press.

20 Use the drill press (or bench vise or quip grip clamp) to press parts together. Don't try to dry fit any of the pieces before final assembly because they don't come apart easily. Press on tip of pen (see photo 22) and clip and cap (see photo 23). Next put the twist mechanism in the top of the lower part of the pen and put this directly under the press, holding it straight up and down (photo 24) and press it in as far as the instructions state (if pressed too far the pen refill will stick out too far). When the mechanism is in place slide the ring on, then put the top part of the pen on, lining up the grain and push on by hand. You don't need to press the top to bottom parts of the pen. The grain should be lined up when the pen is in the closed position.

21 All the pieces needed for the matching pencil (see photo 25) are shown. Instead of pressing in the tip there is a small collar to be pressed in first (see photo 26). Photo 27 shows the clip pressed on. The collar that goes between the top and bottom is being pressed on in photo 27. The pencil, unlike the pen, has to be pressed together. Line up the pattern holding the pencil straight up and down, then press together. Make sure the grain is lined up, before pressing together because you cannot redo this step. Finally put the pencil mechanisim in from the top and screw on the tip (see photo 28).

Note Pen or pencil can be made in different colors and wood patterns. Choose the wood you want and follow the same instructions. Center pen below is made from olivewood and African blackwood.

65

Oak and Cherry Bowl And Goblet

Materials
Oak 1 in x 3 ½ in x 48 in
Cherry ¾ in x 3 ½ in x 48 in

Oak and Cherry Bowl

Procedure

1   For the bowl and goblet I made up a laminate from pallets I found on a construction site (see photo 1). Joint one face and one edge to get a straight and square edge then run them through a thickness planer to get the two faces parallel, and rip the last edge on the table saw about ⅟₃₂ in bigger than the final dimension. Run this edge through the jointer. Now you have two edges and two faces square and parallel to each other.

2   Follow the dimensions (diagram A) and cut all the pieces to size. Remove dust from all surfaces and glue. Note Apply a few beads of glue and spread it with a roller (see photo 2) to speed the gluing process.

3   When all the pieces are glued, clamp together in the same order as in diagram A and allow to set overnight.

4   When dry scrape the glue off one edge and run this edge through the jointer keeping the face against the fence. Trim the other edge at the table saw. This gives a laminate shown in photo 3.

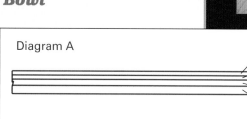

Diagram A
cherry ¼ in x 3½ in x 48 in
oak ¼ in x 3½ in x 48 in
cherry ⅜ in x 3½ in x 48 in
oak ½ in x 3½ in x 48 in

Diagram B
¾ in
21 ³/₁₆ in

5   See diagram B for cutting guide. Photo 4 shows the laminate set up in the table saw. Set the blade to 6° and the fence to 90° to the blade, with a stop block set up to cut ¾ in pieces. Once you've made the first cut flip the laminate over to get the next piece (see diagram B). Cut 30 pieces and number them as you cut so they can be glued back

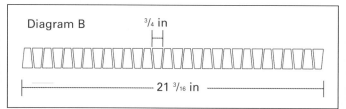

7

Diagram C

¾ in

7 ³/₁₆ in

9

10

12

together in the same order, remembering that every second piece is flipped over. See photos 5 and 6 which shows that every second piece has alternating strips but center strip stays the same. When all pieces are in order tape them together (see photo 5) and then flip them over (see photo 6).

6   Apply a small bead of glue at bottom and top (see photo 7) to ensure the glue will spread evenly along the joint. Applying with a brush takes too long and glue will start to set.

7   Lift the two ends together slowly, allowing glue to spread out. When two ends are together put on the clamps (see photo 8 and diagram C) which have been ready and sized before glue was applied. Note Purchase clamps at any hardware store in plumbing section. They are inexpensive and perfect for gluing bowls and come in sizes 2, 4, 6 inches in diameter and can be put together to get any diameter you need. Allow to dry.

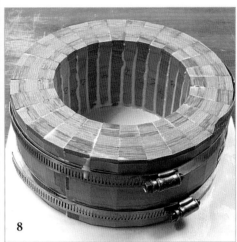

8

8   Make the bottom from cherry, by gluing up a blank 8 in square. Joint the edges of boards and glue them together (see photo 9), keeping the joints even. Photo 10 shows both pieces dry and almost ready for gluing together. Sand the bottom flat using 100 grit paper and a sanding block.

9   Using a straightedge, draw diagonal lines on the bottom to locate the center, then from this mark draw a circle the same size as the bowl. Cut out the bottom on the band saw or a jigsaw.

10   Put the bowl blank in the 4-jaw chuck (see photo 11) and tighten the jaws. Move the tool rest about ¼ in away from the bowl and about center height of the bowl (see photo 12). Using ¼ in parting tool with lathe speed set to low, begin by bringing in the parting tool slowly and perpendicular to the bowl to take off just enough to square the

67

end of the bowl. Check this by laying a straightedge across the end (see photo 13).

11   When both pieces are flat, apply glue to the bottom. While pushing the bowl into the glue, twist back and forth to spread glue evenly until the glue

starts to set. Let this set for a few minutes before applying the clamps (see photo 14) so the bowl and bottom won't move when you clamp it up.

12   Mount bowl on lathe again. Turn on lathe and mark the center. Remove bowl from lathe. From center mark measure ¼ in and mark this with a dot (see photo 15). You will want to mount a 6 in faceplate on this mark (see photos 16 and 17). I made a centering device by turning a piece of hardwood to the same size as the center hole in the faceplate and drilling a hole in the end to fit a small finishing nail. Put the dowel through the faceplate, put the pin on the center mark on the bowl, and slide the faceplate down. This way you have the faceplate perfectly centered on the mark.

13   Secure faceplate to bowl with heavy duty hot melt glue. Wait 15 minutes, then mount it on the lathe. This method works only for small project.

14   The bowl is turned off center to reveal different layers of the laminate at different times producing some interesting patterns.

15   Screw faceplate and bowl onto the lathe and set tool rest ¼ in away from the bowl at center height. Remember the bowl is off center so turn the lathe by hand making sure nothing is hitting.

16   Photo 18 shows the outside of bowl turned until it is round, and bowl set up to turn the inside, with the tool rest set so the tool will cut at center height. I use a tool I made to turn off center projects (see walnut bowl project p82). Bowl is off center so approach the turning bowl with caution.

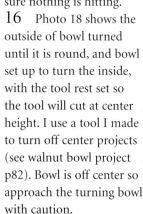

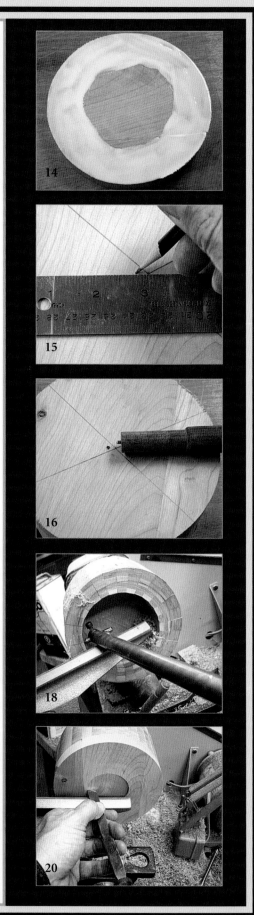

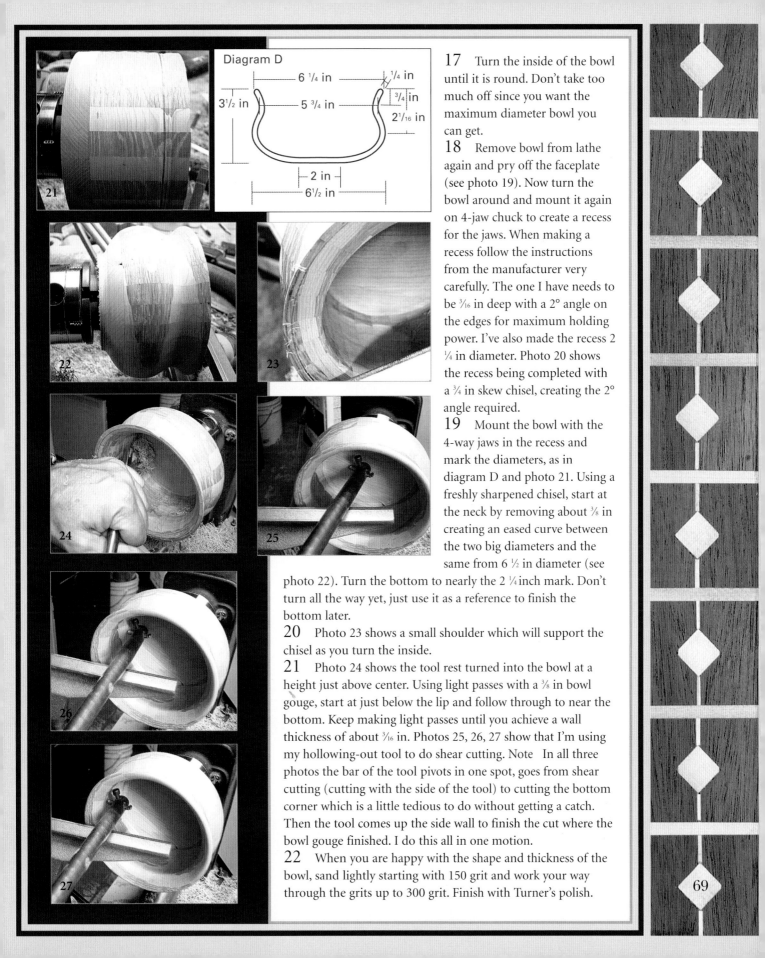

Diagram D

6 ¼ in   ¼ in

3½ in   5 ¾ in   ¾ in

2 ¹⁄₁₆ in

2 in

6½ in

21

22

23

24

25

26

27

17 Turn the inside of the bowl until it is round. Don't take too much off since you want the maximum diameter bowl you can get.

18 Remove bowl from lathe again and pry off the faceplate (see photo 19). Now turn the bowl around and mount it again on 4-jaw chuck to create a recess for the jaws. When making a recess follow the instructions from the manufacturer very carefully. The one I have needs to be ³⁄₁₆ in deep with a 2° angle on the edges for maximum holding power. I've also made the recess 2 ¼ in diameter. Photo 20 shows the recess being completed with a ¾ in skew chisel, creating the 2° angle required.

19 Mount the bowl with the 4-way jaws in the recess and mark the diameters, as in diagram D and photo 21. Using a freshly sharpened chisel, start at the neck by removing about ⅜ in creating an eased curve between the two big diameters and the same from 6 ½ in diameter (see photo 22). Turn the bottom to nearly the 2 ¼ inch mark. Don't turn all the way yet, just use it as a reference to finish the bottom later.

20 Photo 23 shows a small shoulder which will support the chisel as you turn the inside.

21 Photo 24 shows the tool rest turned into the bowl at a height just above center. Using light passes with a ⅜ in bowl gouge, start at just below the lip and follow through to near the bottom. Keep making light passes until you achieve a wall thickness of about ³⁄₁₆ in. Photos 25, 26, 27 show that I'm using my hollowing-out tool to do shear cutting. Note In all three photos the bar of the tool pivots in one spot, goes from shear cutting (cutting with the side of the tool) to cutting the bottom corner which is a little tedious to do without getting a catch. Then the tool comes up the side wall to finish the cut where the bowl gouge finished. I do this all in one motion.

22 When you are happy with the shape and thickness of the bowl, sand lightly starting with 150 grit and work your way through the grits up to 300 grit. Finish with Turner's polish.

23 When the finish is dry remove it from the jaws and switch to the jumbo jaws (see photo 28). Screw on the rubber buttons to the proper diameter and tighten up the jaws just enough to hold the bowl. I used a bowl gouge to remove the recess and tool marks.

28

24 Use the same procedures for sanding as before. Finish sanding the bottom and apply the finish.

Oak and Cherry Goblet

Procedure

1 Use the remaining part of the laminate prepared for the bowl. Leave the fence set at 90° and set the blade to 15°. Cut 12 pieces at ¾ in (see diagram A) and follow the same procedures used in the bowl, first taping and gluing, then clamping (see photos 1 and 2).

2 While this is drying make up a block for the bottom from oak or cherry the same diameter as the top and 4 in long. Let dry, then turn it round. When both pieces are dry, put the top in the 4-way chuck and true up the end (see photo 3).

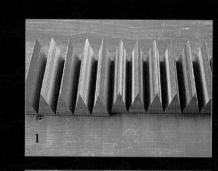

2

3 Leave the top part in the jaws, apply an even amount of glue to both surfaces, and press together while turning.

4 When the glue begins to set bring up the tail stock and apply just enough pressure to hold it in place while the glue dries (see photo 4).

4

5 Photo 5 shows a line drawn up the side of the blank in line with one of the joints at the side of the top. At this location, line up the center finder and draw a line across the blank. Turn the center finder about 90° and draw a second line. The intersection is the center. Now make a mark ¼ in off center and with your spur drive and wooden mallet, hammer in the spur drive to mark this location (see photo 6).

70

Diagram A

¾ in

6¼ in

1

3

5

6

Diagram B

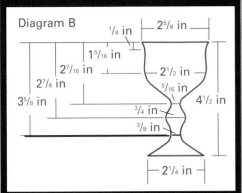

Diagram B

1/4 in
2 5/8 in
1 5/16 in
2 7/16 in
2 7/8 in
2 1/2 in
5/16 in
3 5/8 in
4 1/2 in
3/4 in
3/8 in
2 1/4 in

7

6 Mount the blank on the lathe and bring the tool rest about 1/4 in away and just above center height. Remember you're turning off center so double check the clearance by turning the lathe by hand before starting the lathe. Set the lathe to its slowest speed. Photo 7 shows starting to turn the blank. The leading edge of the gouge is not touching. The bevel should be rubbing before the chisel starts to cut. This ensures that no catches occur when the out-of-round part comes flying around the top of the tool rest.

7 Once the piece is round install a 1 1/4 in Forstner bit in the tail stock and drill in 1 1/2 in, keeping the speed set at slow so the bit won't catch the end grain and throw the blank out of round (see photo 8). Turn the outside to the dimensions in diagram B (see photo 9). Don't turn the stem too narrow yet or the goblet will start to wobble and break.

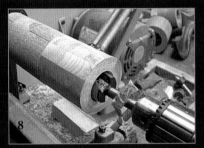

8

9

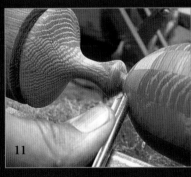

11

12

13

8 Start turning the inside using the bowl gouge. Start just above center with the gouge well over on its side. Start the lathe on slow and remember to keep the bevel rubbing until you are ready to start cutting. Swing the handle of the gouge outwards and this cutting action will leave the surface very smooth, requiring hardly any sanding.

9 While the inside is being turned your index finger is supporting the cup as you get down to the final thickness of 3/16 in or thinner (see photo 10). Try to make the walls of the cup 1/8 in thick In photo 11 the gouge is held at 90° to the rest and the handle down while the bevel is rubbing. Move the handle to the right while rotating to start the cutting action. Always cut from the larger diameter to the smaller diameter to avoid any catches.

10 Photo 12 shows the same procedure working from the larger diameter to the smaller diameter. The bevel is rubbing and in photo 13 as the handle is raised and turned the cutting action begins.

11 In photo 14 use a parting tool to part off the goblet but leave about ½ in to ¾ in for now so the goblet won't wobble.

12 Move aside the tool rest and begin sanding, starting with 150 grit and working through the grits up to 300 grit (see photo 15), making sure that the cup is supported at all times.

13 Once the sanding is complete apply light walnut Danish oil to enhance the grain of the two different woods. Apply a liberal amount of Danish oil with a small brush or cloth and let the finish set for 15 minutes. Apply another liberal coat and let this set for 30 to 60 minutes. With a lint free cloth wipe off any excess oil (final wiping is with the grain). Allow to dry overnight. You may wish to apply another coat. The more coats of

oil applied the more lustrous and harder the surface. Allow each coat to dry for 24 to 48 hrs depending on the humidity (the higher the humidity the longer the oil will take to dry). Note With oil finishes you can also use 0000 steel wool dipped into a small amount of oil. And with the lathe running on low speed you can polish the surface. This works best when the finish has dried for about a week.

14 Photo 16 shows the oil I've put on dripping at the back and collecting in the bottom of the cup. When the finish is dried, use the parting tool to part the remaining part of the goblet. When parting, cradle the goblet in one hand and with the other hand hold the parting tool close to the blade. With the handle tucked under your forearm hold the parting tool firmly and approach the work with the bevel rubbing, raising it until the tool starts to cut, the goblet will fall into your hand.

15 With a sharp chisel take off the little nib left behind from the last step. I first used a ½ in wood chisel (see photo 17). Normally a spindle gouge works better (see photo 18). Sand and finish.

16 To mount the goblet, (photo 19), see the chuck with the worm screw clamped in the 4-way jaws. To use this method, drill the recommended bit diameter in the end of the blank and screw the blank on the chuck making sure the blank is firmly tightened against the jaws.

Segmented Walnut Bowl

Materials
Red oak 1 ¾ in x 2 in x 48 in
Walnut 1 ¾ in x 4 ½ in x 48 in

Procedure
Diagram A shows all the dimensions needed.

Diagram A   First linear laminate

outer
strip

center
strip

outer
strip

———————————————— 47½ in ————————————————

outboard strips

47½ in x 1 in x 1¾ in outboard strips   **47½ in x ¹/₁₆ in x 1¾ in** center strip

47½ in x ¹/₈ in x 1¾ in outer strips

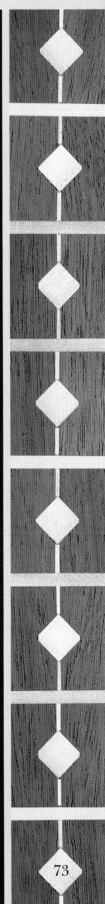

73

1   Walnut strips must be ¹⁄₁₆ in thick. To get this start with strips ⅛ in thick. Tape (double sided) to piece of melamine (see photo 1) and run through thickness planer until smooth. Remove from melamine and repeat process on other side until you get ¹⁄₁₆ in thick. Note Tape comes off the melamine surface easily but not off walnut surface. Use a heat gun to loosen the tape on the walnut. Heat the wood slowly while sliding a putty knife between the walnut and the tape. Strips are ready to glue (see photo 2). Note Remove any glue residue from double sided tape

2   Squeeze out a bead of glue and spread with roller on strips (see photo 3).

3   While gluing strips, stack them in order, as shown in diagram A. Clamp every 4-6 in, making sure that all the pieces are lined up. I made a gluing table to ensure the glued-up pieces are straight (see photo 4). Toggle clamps keep the wood flat on the table. Dry overnight.

4   Remove clamps. Scrape off glue and sand. Do a final clean-up with a thickness planer or sander. Note   Laminate has to be straight, flat, and strips have to be perpendicular to both surfaces (top and bottom). This is essential or design will be mismatched. Before you cut laminate build a sled to help cut segments accurately. See diagram B and following directions at top right.

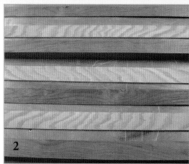

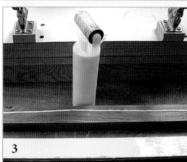

Cut-off Sled

Cut plywood 24 in x 14 in, cut remaining pieces from maple. Fence is 24 in long x 3 in wide x 1 in thick. Support is 17 in long x 4 in wide x 1 ¼ in thick. Runner is cut to fit miter slot in table saw and 14 in long. Drill ¼ in hole in fence and sled at given dimensions. On bottom of sled countersink a one in hole ⅛ in deep. Screw on support in upper left corner of sled using 1 ½ in screws (2 screws on either side of blade to ensure that sled will stay even when you cut through support and sled, and that laminate will stay flat when cutting. Put the two screws on right side of blade far enough so tilted saw blade won't hit screws. Make runner to fit miter slot, not too tight, it must slide smoothly (sand runner to fit or apply dry lubricant between table and sled) in miter slot. Measure from the right side of sled 13 ¹¹⁄₁₆ in. Line this mark up with center of left miter slot and then slide table saw fence over to left side of sled to keep the sled square to the blade while attaching the runner with ¾ in screws. Attach the fence. From bottom of sled slide in 2 in carriage bolt through sled and fence using a washer and nut. Note   To adjust angle on fence, tighten the nut to secure the fence. To make multiple cuts put in a screw at either end of the fence.

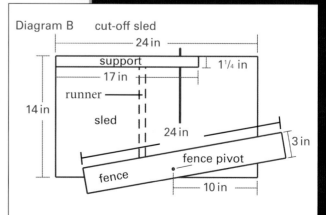

Diagram B   cut-off sled

Diagram C

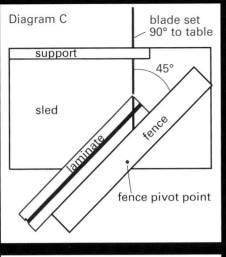

blade set 90° to table

support

sled

45°

laminate

fence

fence pivot point

Diagram D

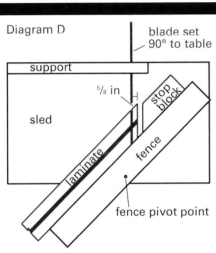

blade set 90° to table

support

⅝ in

stop block

sled

laminate

fence

fence pivot point

Diagram E — Second linear laminate

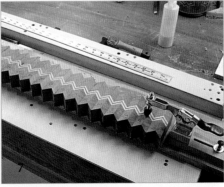

trim off at these points

turn over every other segment end over end to reveal the second linear laminate

5 To cut laminate set the fence to 45° and the blade 90° to the table (see diagram C). Line the corner of the laminate to the blade. Clamp in place and cut the corner off. Using a stop block measure and clamp the stop block so you will get ⅝ in segments. Number segments as you cut so they can be glued back in the same order (see diagram D).

6 Then sand each segment lightly, removing all splinters. Line up all segments in order, flip every second one end over end to reveal the second linear laminate (see diagram E).

7 To glue segments into the second linear laminate start by gluing two segments together, then glue two of these into fours and two of these into eights to get second laminate (see diagram E). While gluing *keep the pattern straight.* Note When gluing apply a small amount of glue to each surface, hold the pieces together and slide them back and forth to spread the glue evenly. As glue starts to set, align the pattern on both sides. Set aside for a few minutes, then clamp (clamping too soon will make them slide around).

8 Once the second laminate is finished the points have to be trimmed off (see diagram E and photo 5). Start by measuring and marking from the design to the edge of the laminate on both edges and on both sides. The object is to have an equal amount of wood on both sides of the design. Transfer this mark onto the end of laminate (see photo 6).

9 Trim off the points using a jig (see photo 7). To build the jig follow the steps

5

6

7

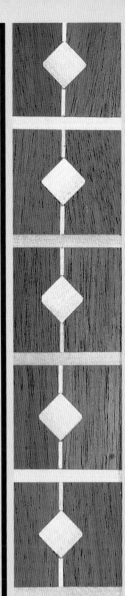

75

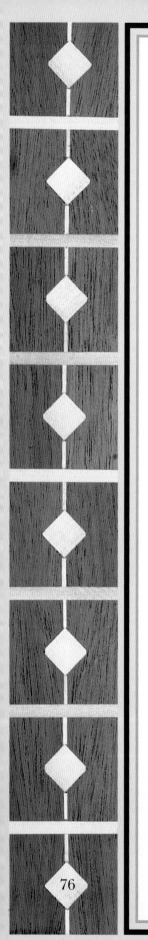

in diagram F (ripping sled and base for toggle clamps).

10 Line up the mark made on the edge of the laminate with the edge of the jig (see photo 6).

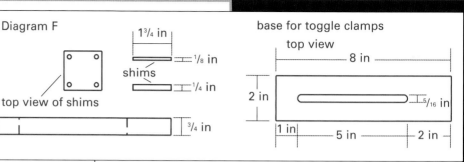

Diagram F

top view of shims

shims

1¾ in

⅛ in

¼ in

¾ in

base for toggle clamps

top view

8 in

2 in

⁵⁄₁₆ in

1 in   5 in   2 in

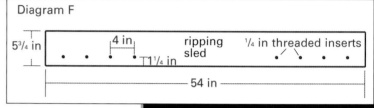

Diagram F

5¾ in

4 in

1¼ in

ripping sled

¼ in threaded inserts

54 in

Clamp the laminate with toggle clamps (see photo 7). Keeping the fence set at 5 ¾ in, raise the blade so 2 to 3 teeth are above the top of the laminate. Carefully push the laminate through the blade. Be sure to wear safety glasses and gloves when doing this procedure.

11 To find the center of design (see photo 8) use a compass and sharp pencil. Put point of compass on glue line in the middle of the walnut strip and set the compass so the marks meet. (Pencil marks are enhanced with a fine tip marker for clarity.) Photo 9 shows a line drawn through these points at 45°. Photo 10 shows every second one of these marks along the edge of the laminate. On the opposite edge of the laminate, mark the ones you didn't on the first edge. Now mark a center line the length of the laminate (see photo 10) on both edges to find where to make the cuts. The intersection on the edge of the laminate is where the blade will pass through.

12 After marking the 18 segments (Each segment is the distance between the marks made earlier with the compass) the formula for finding the angle of the blade is the circumference (360) divided by the number of segments (18) divided by 2 (miter) or 360 divide by 18 divide by 2 =10°. Note   You can replace 18 in the formula with the number of segments you have in any project.

13 Photo 12 shows the elaborate sled with a laser that I made to cut the segments; however, this sled is not needed unless you plan to cut many segmented bowls. Instead, use the cut-off sled described on p74. The laser in photos 11 and 12 shows where the blade will cut. If you don't have a laser set your square to 10° and draw a line through the intersecting lines shown by the laser line. Note   The laser does not follow the lines. These lines are only to find the intersection where you want to make the cut.

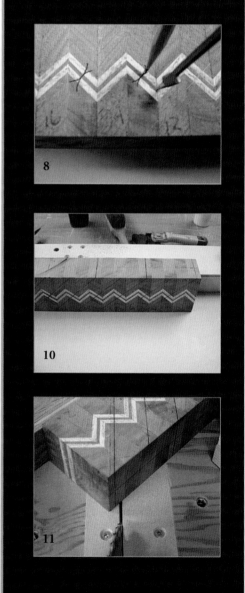

8

9

10

11

Diagram G

blade set 90° to table

support

first cut through D point

sled

45°

fence

fence pivot point

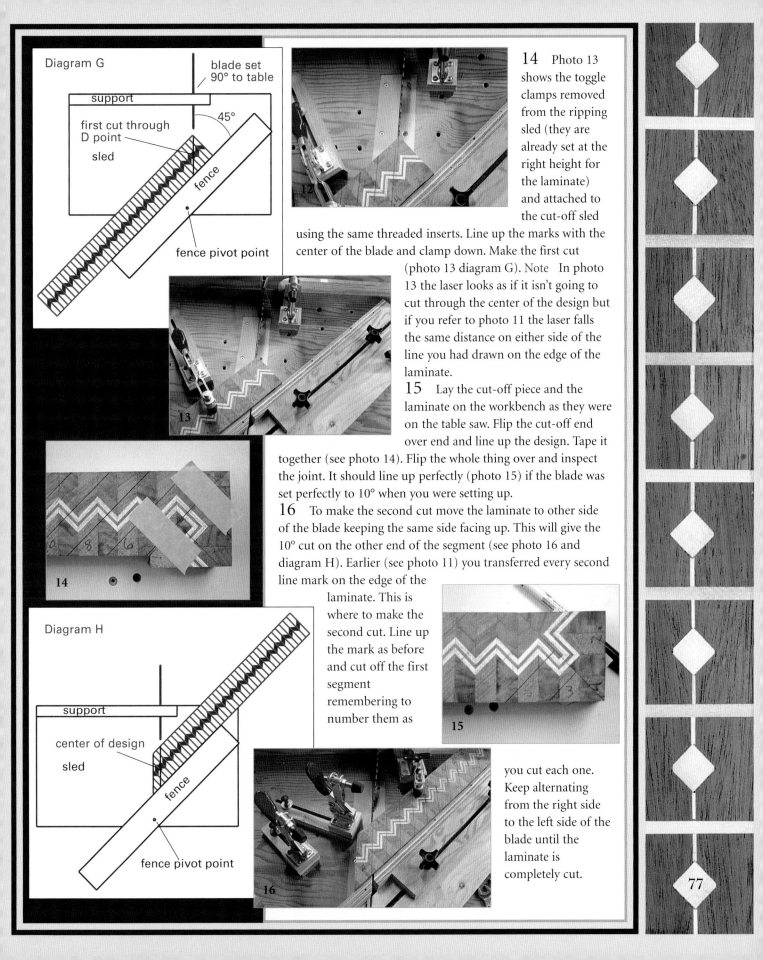

12

13

14

14 Photo 13 shows the toggle clamps removed from the ripping sled (they are already set at the right height for the laminate) and attached to the cut-off sled using the same threaded inserts. Line up the marks with the center of the blade and clamp down. Make the first cut (photo 13 diagram G). Note In photo 13 the laser looks as if it isn't going to cut through the center of the design but if you refer to photo 11 the laser falls the same distance on either side of the line you had drawn on the edge of the laminate.

15 Lay the cut-off piece and the laminate on the workbench as they were on the table saw. Flip the cut-off end over end and line up the design. Tape it together (see photo 14). Flip the whole thing over and inspect the joint. It should line up perfectly (photo 15) if the blade was set perfectly to 10° when you were setting up.

16 To make the second cut move the laminate to other side of the blade keeping the same side facing up. This will give the 10° cut on the other end of the segment (see photo 16 and diagram H). Earlier (see photo 11) you transferred every second line mark on the edge of the laminate. This is where to make the second cut. Line up the mark as before and cut off the first segment remembering to number them as

15

you cut each one. Keep alternating from the right side to the left side of the blade until the laminate is completely cut.

Diagram H

support

center of design

sled

fence

fence pivot point

16

17 Flip end over end every second segment to create the new pattern (photo 17). There is a gap between the segments at the bottom if everything was cut correctly. These joints will close in the next steps.

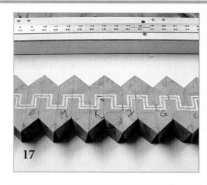

18 Before gluing, tape all the pieces together. Begin by lining up two of the segments, keep them tightly together, put a piece of tape above and below the pattern. Keep the pattern visible and lined up until all the segments are taped together (photo 18).

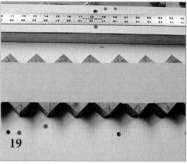

Apply 3 or 4 layers of tape (photo 19) to the remainder of the surface to keep the segments aligned in the succeeding steps.

19 Before applying glue, do a dry fit. Carefully turn the laminate over, tape side down. Bring the ends of the laminate together matching the pattern. The design should match up on the inside and outside of the bowl and all the joints should be tight. Note If the joints do not fit properly check accuracy of fence and blade set-up.

20 Do not spread glue on the surface (photo 20) of the segments. Apply a small bead at the bottom of the joint. The tape will keep the glue from seeping out. Then glue the edges of the segments at either end and lift both ends together slowly to allow the glue to spread out. Note If this step is done too quickly the tape may break. Match up the pattern on the last two pieces (photo 21), then tape above and below the design (see photo 22).

21 The last joint (photo 21) doesn't line up very well but will come together nicely when clamps are tightened. To clamp bowls I use hose clamps that plumbers use to join pipes (purchase at any home center). Use two clamps, one above and one below the pattern. When tightening the clamps apply just enough pressure to close all the joints (photo 22) and tighten each clamp a little at a time for even pressure. Dry overnight.

22 Clean up the outside of the bowl by removing all tape and glue.

23 Photo 23 shows jig to clamp down the bowl to cut the top and bottom parallel to the design on the bowl. To build the jig (diagram J) use a piece of plywood 9 ½ in x 24 in x ¼ in thick for the base, cut the runner to fit the miter slot on the band saw

78

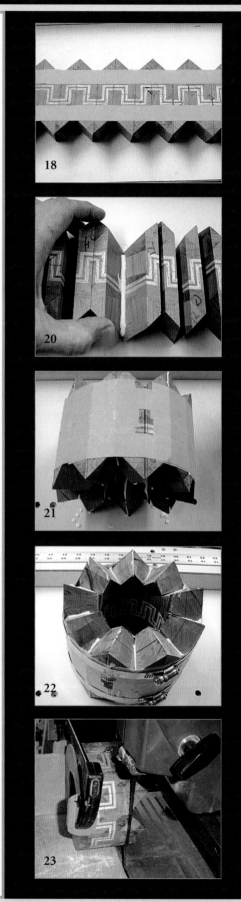

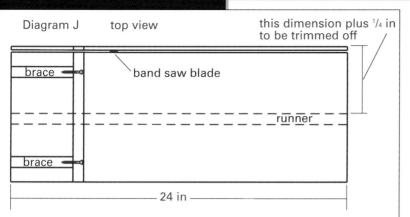

Diagram J   top view

this dimension plus ¼ in
to be trimmed off

brace

band saw blade

runner

brace

24 in

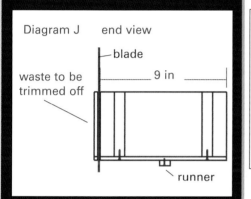

Diagram J   end view

blade

waste to be
trimmed off

9 in

runner

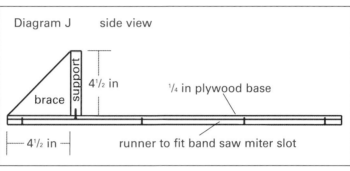

Diagram J   side view

support

4½ in

brace

¼ in plywood base

4½ in

runner to fit band saw miter slot

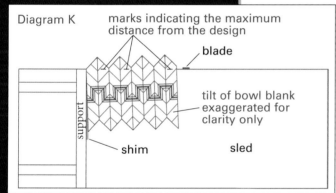

Diagram K

marks indicating the maximum
distance from the design

blade

support

tilt of bowl blank
exaggerated for
clarity only

shim

sled

and attach the runner to the base with ½ in screws the distance between blade and miter slot plus ½ in you'll trim off after the jig is built. From ¾ in material cut the support and braces and attach them with 1 ¼ in screws according to diagram J. Put the finished sled in the miter slot, turn on the band saw, and trim off edge of the sled making sure that the blade is set perfectly to 90°. This edge becomes the reference when setting up to cut the bowl.

24   To get marks in diagram K measure the maximum distance from the design to the points. Line up the marks with the edge of the sled, support, and blade. Now clamp the bowl on the sled and slide the jig and the bowl up to the blade with the band saw turned off. One of the marks should line up with blade (see photo 23). If not slide a shim between the bowl and the support as in diagram K.

25   Cut off points, on top and bottom. You should now have a bowl blank where the top and bottom are parallel to the each other and to the design. Sand off the band saw marks. Mount the bowl on the lathe and turn the top and bottom flat by using a parting tool (photo 24). By laying a ruler across the bottom of the bowl you can tell when the top and bottom are flat (photo 25).

24

25

79

26 Using ¾ in scrap material (see photo 26) make a blank for the bottom (measure the diameter of the bowl). Apply an even amount of glue to all edges and clamp. Sandwich blank between two pieces of melamine, put on two horizontal clamps to pull the joints together. Dry overnight (see photo 27).

26

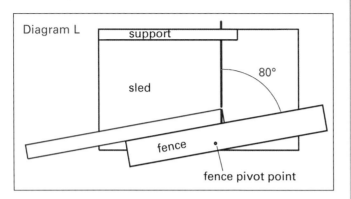

Diagram L

support

sled

80°

fence

fence pivot point

27

27 To make rings, use two strips oak and one walnut ⅛ in x 1 ⅝ in x 24 in. Set miter sled fence to 10° and the blade to 90° (see photo 28 and diagram L). Set up a stop block so the segment measures ¾ in against the fence (see photo 29 and diagram M). Cut 18 segments and number them as you cut. Put them together to form a ring. The

28

29

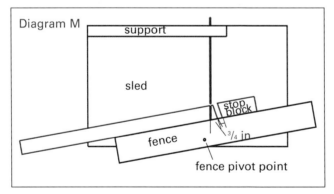

Diagram M

support

sled

stop block

fence

³/₄ in

fence pivot point

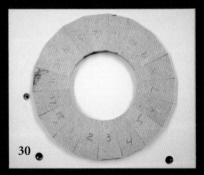

30

joints should fit tight (see photo 30) without any pressure. Note   There is no way to clamp these pieces because they are thin. If the joints don't fit tightly reset the fence until they do. Once you are satisfied with the joints cut 54 pieces from oak (3 rings) and 36 pieces from walnut (2 rings). See photo 31.

31

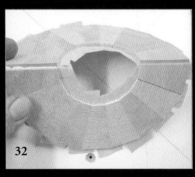

32

80

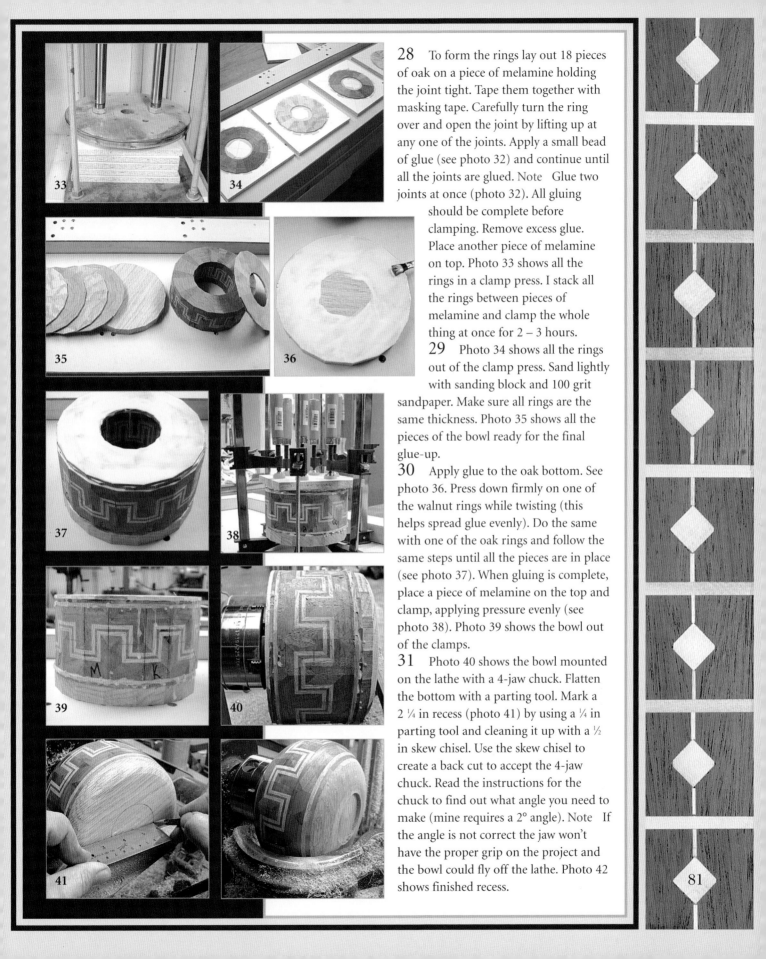

28 To form the rings lay out 18 pieces of oak on a piece of melamine holding the joint tight. Tape them together with masking tape. Carefully turn the ring over and open the joint by lifting up at any one of the joints. Apply a small bead of glue (see photo 32) and continue until all the joints are glued. Note   Glue two joints at once (photo 32). All gluing should be complete before clamping. Remove excess glue. Place another piece of melamine on top. Photo 33 shows all the rings in a clamp press. I stack all the rings between pieces of melamine and clamp the whole thing at once for 2 – 3 hours.

29 Photo 34 shows all the rings out of the clamp press. Sand lightly with sanding block and 100 grit sandpaper. Make sure all rings are the same thickness. Photo 35 shows all the pieces of the bowl ready for the final glue-up.

30 Apply glue to the oak bottom. See photo 36. Press down firmly on one of the walnut rings while twisting (this helps spread glue evenly). Do the same with one of the oak rings and follow the same steps until all the pieces are in place (see photo 37). When gluing is complete, place a piece of melamine on the top and clamp, applying pressure evenly (see photo 38). Photo 39 shows the bowl out of the clamps.

31 Photo 40 shows the bowl mounted on the lathe with a 4-jaw chuck. Flatten the bottom with a parting tool. Mark a 2 ¼ in recess (photo 41) by using a ¼ in parting tool and cleaning it up with a ½ in skew chisel. Use the skew chisel to create a back cut to accept the 4-jaw chuck. Read the instructions for the chuck to find out what angle you need to make (mine requires a 2° angle). Note   If the angle is not correct the jaw won't have the proper grip on the project and the bowl could fly off the lathe. Photo 42 shows finished recess.

32 To shape the bowl turn the bowl round to its maximum diameter and gradually round the bottom over to the recess you made, staying about ¼ in away. Photo 43 shows the bowl curved towards the chuck. I removed just enough to visually see the balance of the bowl.

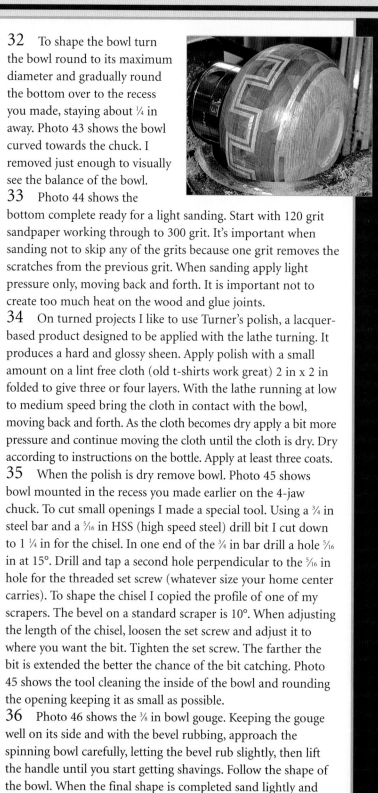

44

45

46

33 Photo 44 shows the bottom complete ready for a light sanding. Start with 120 grit sandpaper working through to 300 grit. It's important when sanding not to skip any of the grits because one grit removes the scratches from the previous grit. When sanding apply light pressure only, moving back and forth. It is important not to create too much heat on the wood and glue joints.

34 On turned projects I like to use Turner's polish, a lacquer-based product designed to be applied with the lathe turning. It produces a hard and glossy sheen. Apply polish with a small amount on a lint free cloth (old t-shirts work great) 2 in x 2 in folded to give three or four layers. With the lathe running at low to medium speed bring the cloth in contact with the bowl, moving back and forth. As the cloth becomes dry apply a bit more pressure and continue moving the cloth until the cloth is dry. Dry according to instructions on the bottle. Apply at least three coats.

35 When the polish is dry remove bowl. Photo 45 shows bowl mounted in the recess you made earlier on the 4-jaw chuck. To cut small openings I made a special tool. Using a ¾ in steel bar and a ⁵⁄₁₆ in HSS (high speed steel) drill bit I cut down to 1 ¼ in for the chisel. In one end of the ¾ in bar drill a hole ⁵⁄₁₆ in at 15°. Drill and tap a second hole perpendicular to the ⁵⁄₁₆ in hole for the threaded set screw (whatever size your home center carries). To shape the chisel I copied the profile of one of my scrapers. The bevel on a standard scraper is 10°. When adjusting the length of the chisel, loosen the set screw and adjust it to where you want the bit. Tighten the set screw. The farther the bit is extended the better the chance of the bit catching. Photo 45 shows the tool cleaning the inside of the bowl and rounding the opening keeping it as small as possible.

36 Photo 46 shows the ⅜ in bowl gouge. Keeping the gouge well on its side and with the bevel rubbing, approach the spinning bowl carefully, letting the bevel rub slightly, then lift the handle until you start getting shavings. Follow the shape of the bowl. When the final shape is completed sand lightly and apply the finish as described above.

83

Maple Leaf Bowl

Materials

Holly ¾ in x ¾ in in x 80 in
Bloodwood ¾ in x ¾ in in x 80 in

Procedure

1 Make all the pieces in diagram A using a jointer and thickness planer. Cut the outboard and center strip from bloodwood and the two outer strips from holly.

2 Once pieces are cut, dust all edges and sides of all strips, and apply glue to both mating edges of all the strips (see photo 1). Note I prefer to apply a bead of glue and spread it with a roller to speed up gluing process since the glue sets in 20 minutes.

3 Clamp freshly glued linear laminate (see photo 2) on a clamping table. Build a clamping/gluing table 5 ft long from ¾ in plywood and glue on a cover of plastic laminate for easy clean-up. Make it flat with a straight clamping edge to keep the laminate flat and straight. When you're cutting the laminate on the table saw the wood must lie flat. Otherwise the pattern won't line up. Use toggle clamps to hold the linear laminate tight to the table and F clamps to hold it to the fence.

4 When glue has dried remove any excess from both sides of the laminate using a 2 in scraper (see photo 3).

5 Set up the cut-off sled (see diagram B). Set fence to 45° to the blade and set the blade 90° to the table. Cut off corner of the linear laminate, then set up a stop block to get ½ in segments (an 80 in piece of laminate should yield 80 segments).

6 When the first segment is cut off flip it over end and match up the pattern (see photo 4). Note The design should match on both top and bottom surfaces of laminate. If not the blade was not set exactly to 90° to the table. Reset the blade and try again until design matches. Now cut all the pieces.

7 Before you start gluing, flip every second piece end over end (see photo 5). Glue the single segments into double segments

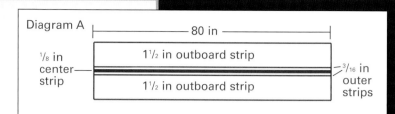

Diagram A

	80 in
⅛ in center strip	1½ in outboard strip
	1½ in outboard strip

³⁄₁₆ in outer strips

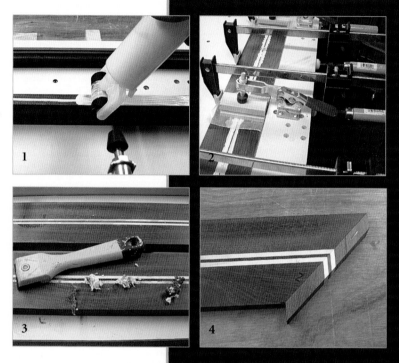

Diagram B

set blade to 90°

support

½ in

45°

sled

fence

fence pivot point

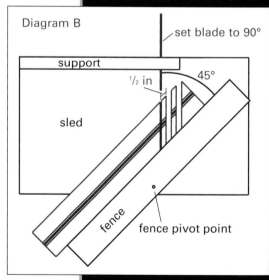

1

2

3

4

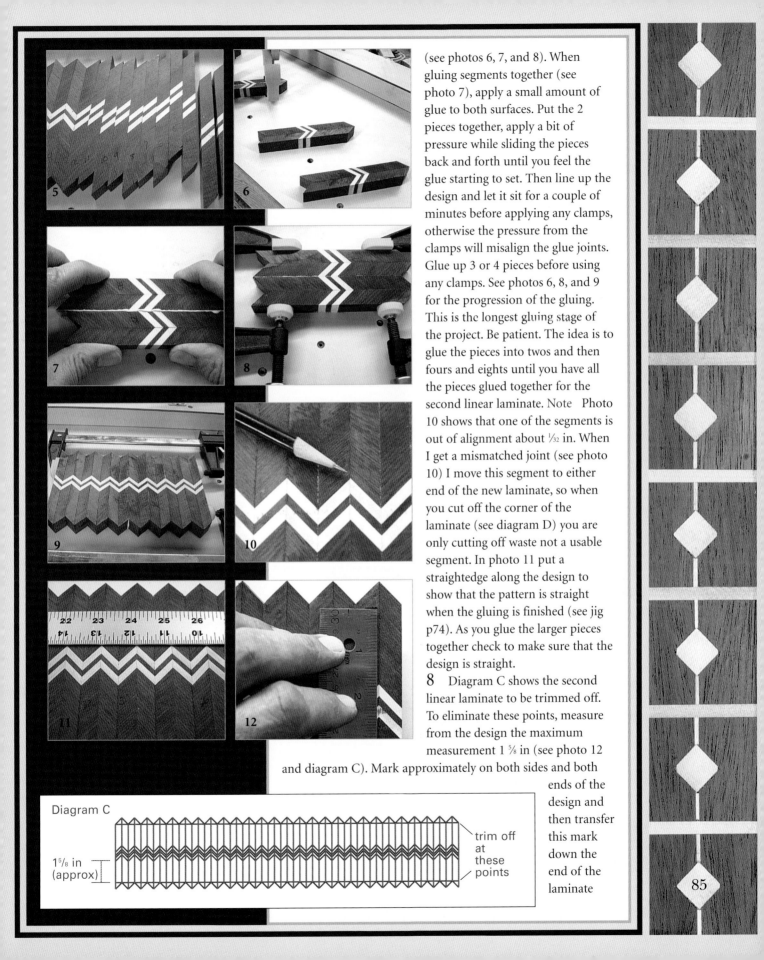

(see photos 6, 7, and 8). When gluing segments together (see photo 7), apply a small amount of glue to both surfaces. Put the 2 pieces together, apply a bit of pressure while sliding the pieces back and forth until you feel the glue starting to set. Then line up the design and let it sit for a couple of minutes before applying any clamps, otherwise the pressure from the clamps will misalign the glue joints. Glue up 3 or 4 pieces before using any clamps. See photos 6, 8, and 9 for the progression of the gluing. This is the longest gluing stage of the project. Be patient. The idea is to glue the pieces into twos and then fours and eights until you have all the pieces glued together for the second linear laminate. Note Photo 10 shows that one of the segments is out of alignment about ¹⁄₃₂ in. When I get a mismatched joint (see photo 10) I move this segment to either end of the new laminate, so when you cut off the corner of the laminate (see diagram D) you are only cutting off waste not a usable segment. In photo 11 put a straightedge along the design to show that the pattern is straight when the gluing is finished (see jig p74). As you glue the larger pieces together check to make sure that the design is straight.

8   Diagram C shows the second linear laminate to be trimmed off. To eliminate these points, measure from the design the maximum measurement 1 ⁵⁄₈ in (see photo 12 and diagram C). Mark approximately on both sides and both ends of the design and then transfer this mark down the end of the laminate

Diagram C

1⁵⁄₈ in
(approx)

trim off
at
these
points

85

(see photo 13). Line up the mark with the edge of the ripping sled, and using the toggle clamps, clamp the laminate down (see photo 14). Set the fence on the table saw to cut off the tips (see photo 15). Turn the laminate around and do the same to the other side.

9 To find the center of the design, place a compass in the center of the center stripe on the descending leg of the design (see photo 16) and draw two arcs that intersect in the middle. Then draw a line through the intersection at a 60° angle (see photo 17). This is the line used to line up the center of the blade (see photo 18). Cut all the segments. Photo 19 shows that with the toggle clamps adjusted you can safely cut to the end of the laminate.

10 Photo 20 shows gluing again. Follow the same steps described on p85 making sure you keep the design straight with a straightedge (see photo 21).

11 Measure and cut off the tips (see photo 22). Note Measurements given in diagram E for this step are approximate and might vary by ⅛ in depending on your accuracy cutting strips and outboard pieces.

12 With a compass mark the arcs again using the same procedure as above and again draw a 60° angle through the arcs (see photo 23). Note Photo 23 also shows that at

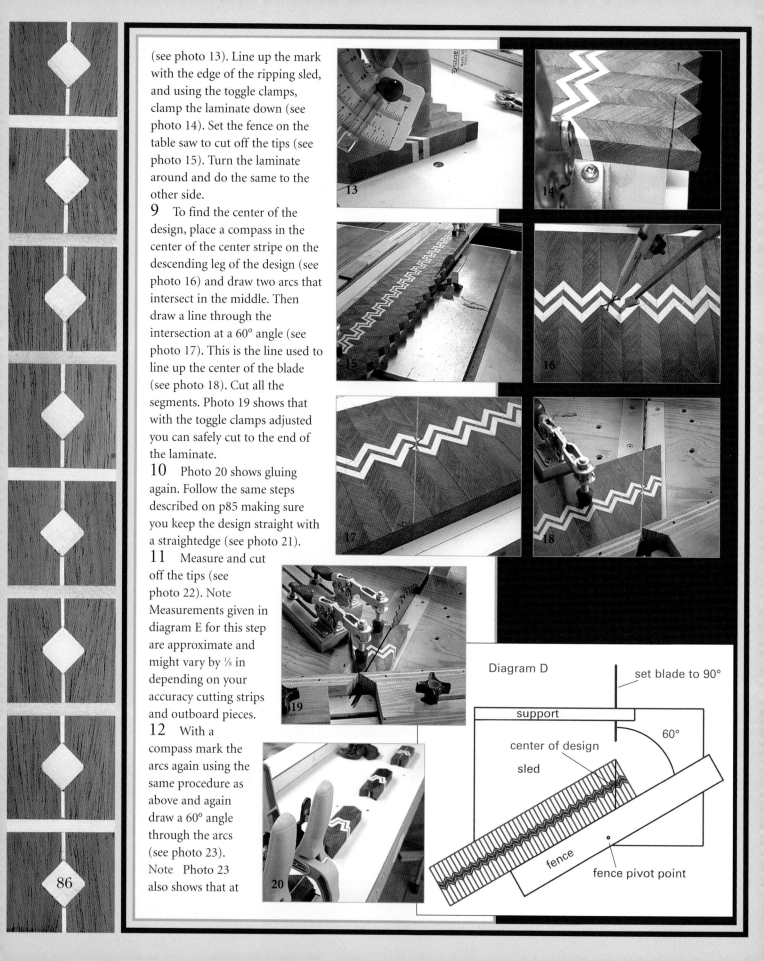

13

14

15

16

17

18

19

20

Diagram D

set blade to 90°

support

60°

center of design

sled

fence

fence pivot point

86

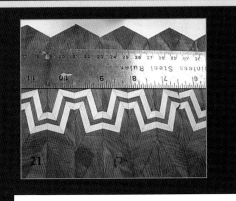

21

22

every second mark I drew the line to the opposite side of the laminate. Also notice that all the marks are on the descending part of the design.

13 From this mark, square a line across the

Diagram E

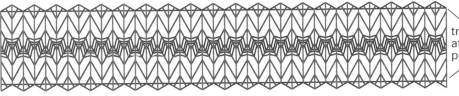

1 11/16 in (approx)

trim off at these points

23

24

edge and then draw a line in the middle of laminate (see photo 24). Once every second mark is squared on both edges it's time to make the final cuts.

Note Unfortunately it's a compound miter. It sounds difficult, but should be managed without much trouble.

14 Photo 25 is taken from the back of the table saw. In photo 25 and diagram F the laminate is set up to the right of the blade. Draw a line 11 1/4° on an angle to indicate the tilt of the blade. This angled line doesn't intersect the line drawn earlier on the face of the laminate to cut the segments.

Diagram F

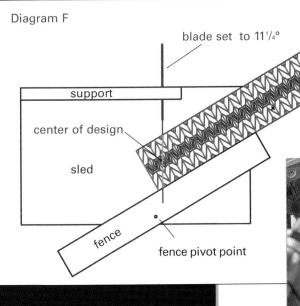

blade set to 11 1/4°

support

center of design

sled

fence

fence pivot point

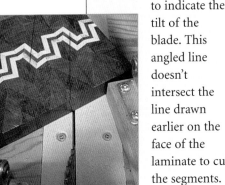

25

87

Photo 26 shows every second line in action.

15 Make the first cut, then flip the newly cut segment end over end and see if the design matches as you did in photo 4. If it does continue to flip the laminate over to the left side of the blade (see photo 27) and (diagram G). As you did previously, draw the angled line (see photo 25) to assist in lining up the blade. Remember that the only line drawn at 11 ¼° on the edge of the laminate is to be lined up with the center of the blade. The other lines were to get this intersection. Note Before I commit to cutting the laminate I take a scrap piece of wood and cut equal size pieces to make sure that the fence and blade are set correctly. Be sure to number segments so you can glue them back together in order.

16 When all the segments are cut it is time for the final glue-up. Line all the segments in order flipping every second segment end over end, lining up the design and taping them together (see photo 28), covering the entire laminate with tape so they won't slide out of alignment. Flip it over. Trial fit by bringing the two ends together and putting on the plumber's clamps (see photo 29). If there are any mismatches adjust them by twisting the segments in and out or being more accurate setting up fence and blade. Note When you're satisfied with the match proceed with gluing. Apply a small bead of glue shown in photo 30 and then the clamps (see photo 29). Allow to dry overnight.

17 Make up the rings by cutting a piece of holly ³⁄₁₆ in x ⅞ in x 48 in and a piece of bloodwood ³⁄₁₆ in x ⅞ in x 24 in using the same method as for the stripes of the walnut bowl. Set up the blade to 90° and the fence at 11.25, then measure over 1 ⁵⁄₁₆ in from the blade and clamp a stop block (see photo 31). Use an awl to hold the small

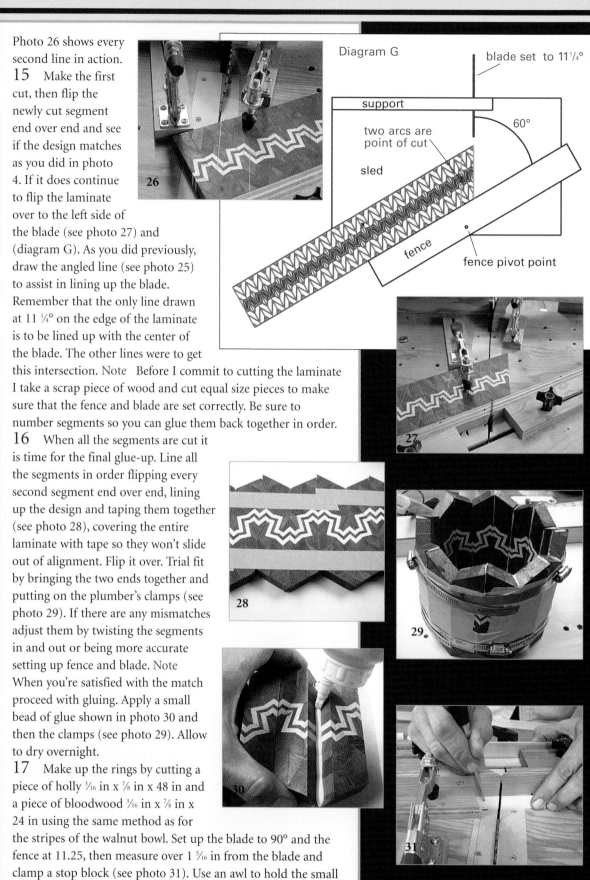

Diagram G

blade set to 11 ¼°

support

60°

two arcs are
point of cut

sled

fence

fence pivot point

26

27

28

29

30

31

pieces in place. Cut 16 pieces from bloodwood and 32 pieces from holly.

18 Glue the rings together and hold the pieces together with masking tape (see photo 32). When applying the glue lift one edge of the ring and apply a small bead at the bottom of the joint (glue two joints at once with this method, see photo 33). Photo also shows gluing each ring on top of a piece of melamine. When gluing is finished put another piece of melamine on top of ring and clamp (use clamps or a clamp press) as in the walnut bowl project (see p81).

19 Make up a bottom from bloodwood (7 ¼ in x 7 ¼ in x ¾ in, see photo 34). Make six pieces 7 ¼ in x 1 ¼ in to make up the blank (see photo 34). Glue and clamp and let dry overnight.

20 Remove clamps and tape from bowl. Note I used band saw for walnut bowl, this time I used table saw to cut off the tips. First sand the top or bottom of the blank on a piece of 80 grit sandpaper glued to ¾ in plywood. Sand just enough so the bowl doesn't rock back and forth (see photo 35).

21 Build another jig 24 in long 8 in high and 8 in wide (see photo 36). It should be parallel to the fence and the vertical supports should be exactly 90° to the table. Set the fence and the jig so the blade will cut off just the tips. To use the jig hold the bowl tight against the fence (not the table) on the side you just sanded so it doesn't rock, raise the blade to 1 ½ in and start pushing slowly through the blade of table saw. Be sure that you've cleared the blade before lifting the bowl. For the second cut turn the bowl ¼ turn and repeat these steps. When finished reset the fence and turn the bowl around and repeat for the other side of the bowl.

22 If you have any saw marks when you're finished cutting, sand with 80 grit paper and a sanding block.

23 From the blank you made earlier for the bottom, use your band saw and cut a 7 ¼ in diameter circle. Photo 37 shows all the pieces ready for final glue-up. Follow the steps for walnut bowl to glue and assemble (see p81). To clamp, put a piece of melamine on the top so the clamps will distribute even pressure (see photo 38). Let dry overnight.

24 To mount the bowl use the 4-jaw chuck with the small jaws

32

33

34

35

36

37

38

39

89

replaced by the jumbo jaws, installed with the rubber buttons (see photo 39). The rubber buttons have a secure grip on the rings that are hanging over the bowl. If not secure enough bring up the tailstock. From this point the only tool I use is the ⅜ in bowl gouge, which I use for virtually everything. I prefer to keep the shape fairly simple to emphasize the design and the contrast of the woods.

25   First flatten the bottom and create a recess for the jaws according to the manufacturer's instructions. Round the bottom of bowl (see photo 40).

26   Start to sand with 120 grit paper and go up to 320 grit paper. Apply 2 to 3 coats of Turner's polish as described in the earlier projects. When dry remove the bowl and jumbo jaws and replace with the small jaws. Mount the bowl in the recess (see photo 41).

27   Turn the same shape on the top of the bowl then start turning the inside. I used the bowl gouge. Adjust the tool rest about ¼ in away from the bowl so the gouge will cut at just above center. Refer to oak cherry bowl project for a clear photo (see p68). Note   When turning bowls or other projects I try to achieve a minimum of ³⁄₁₆ in to ¼ in wall thickness or thinner if possible. This project has wall thickness slightly less than ¼ in. Bloodwood is very hard and I had to sharpen my gouge about every 3 to 4 minutes. Residue builds up on the gouge from heat generated by friction. Wipe the gouge off with lacquer thinners as needed to alleviate this problem.

Helpful Hints for laminating

1   Before you cut your laminate, joint and surface a piece of scrap lumber.

2   For measuring angles I found a sliding protractor in the drafting section of an office supply store. It is very accurate (see photo 13 and photo 28 in walnut bowl project). Even so I always test cut on some MDF (medium density fiberboard). Cut pieces into 2 in strips and have a few of these strips on hand for setting up. Photos 42 and 43 show how close the joints should fit. I've used transparent tape to hold them together. Photo 42 shows that when the fence is set at 45° only 4 test pieces were needed. But in photo 43 when the fence was set to 11.25°, 16 pieces were needed. When fitting these test pieces together they should fit without any pressure being applied for a good looking joint.

40

41

42

43

Candlesticks

Materials
Candlestick Oak ¾ in x ¾ in x 80 in
Leaves   Oak, bloodwood, padauk,
pau amarillo, walnut

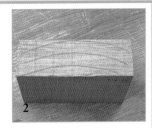

Procedure

1   These candlesticks were made from an old Manitoba oak tree, felled in our back yard. Use a wood of your choice. Make candlesticks in your choice of style. Mine are 3 in diameter and 29 in high. They will be trimmed with branches and leaves.

2   Cut six ¼ in x ¼ in strips of oak and round them off using a drum sander in your drill. They should look like branches. Soak the strips in hot water for 2 to 3 hours (bath tub works great) to make them pliable enough to bend around a 3 in plastic pipe which is the size of my candlesticks.

3   Make a simple jig for the pipe (see photo 1). Turn a piece of wood to the same diameter as the inside of the pipe. Screw this in the center of a piece of plywood 8 in x 8 in and slide the pipe over the disk and screw the pipe to the disk. Then clamp the jig to your workbench. Clamp the wet strips at one end to the pipe using surgical tubing (I purchased a 6 ft piece at a local hardware store). Begin at the bottom by pulling the tubing tight while twisting the branch around the pipe (see photo 1). Clamp and twist 2 or 3 at once and leave them in this clamped position for at least 3 days so the branches don't untwist when you remove the tubing.

4   To make the leaves, cut some blocks 2 ¾ in x 1 ¾ in and draw (see photo 2) some arcs (I used a one gallon paint can for the arcs) and cut these out on the band saw. Photo 3 shows a few different size templates for the leaves, which you can make any size.

5   Begin to carve out the middle of the leaf (see photo 4) using the bit (see photo 5) in the middle of the bottom row.

This bit removes the wood quickly but the cut remaining is very rough. To smooth it out I started with the spurred bit in photo 5 far left on the bottom row. This bit is good for general sanding and for blending all the contours required for making leaves and for finish sanding. I use a combination of the two drum sanders with a different grit of paper on each one. For the final sanding I use the flap wheel (see photo 6) .

6   When gluing the leaves, contour the end of the stem of each leaf to fit the branch. The closer the fit the better it looks.

7 When the glue has set start to blend the stem and branch together.

8 Use the CA glue (instant glue) and accelerator to glue stems to branches. Once you are satisfied with the fit apply a small amount of glue to the stem and hold it in place with your third hand. Then spray the joint with the accelerator. It takes only seconds to dry. Note Wear gloves or have some lacquer thinner close by because this glue will glue your fingers together more quickly than it glues the wood. The accelerator turns the glue white (see photo 7). Take it off with a bit in the dremel tool (see photo 5).

9 When all the glue has set and dried, further blending may be done. Apply a very small amount of yellow glue with a toothpick to the joint. Allow the glue to skin over, then with your sanding attachments in the dremel tool begin to sand the joints. The glue will mix with the sawdust and further fill any gaps and conceal the joints. When all the blending and sanding are complete, apply a finish. I used a gloss spray Varathane. Apply in very thin coats so you don't cause any runs or sags while you cover the front and back of all the leaves.

Note When tracing the leaf pattern (I used a leaf from one of my wife's plants) on the block of wood, orient the pattern so the length of the leaf is with the grain of the wood (otherwise the stem may break off in the carving process). When deciding on the shape of a leaf it is really up to the individual.

Helpful Hint You don't need to steam the small strips to bend them. Soaking them in hot water works as well. To get the proper diameter of the pipe to match the diameter of your project, choose pipe that is ½ in to 1 in smaller than the project because when you take the strips out of the clamps they will always untwist somewhat. The pipe should be at least as high as the project. Every species of wood has its own characteristics, so judge accordingly. Make a few extra pieces of wood for bending, because some are going to break during the process.

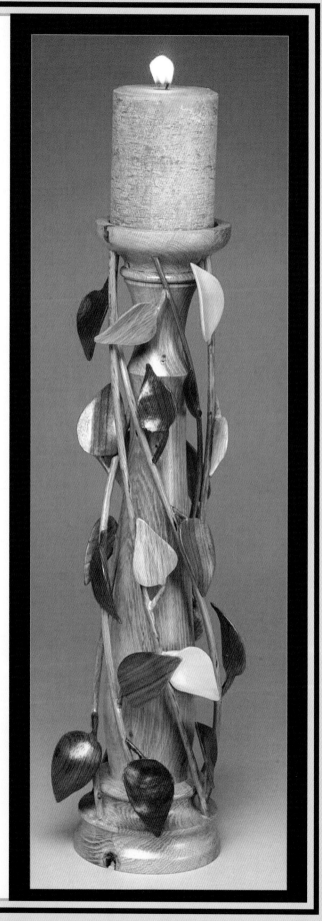

Kaleidoscope Plate

Materials
Wood scraps

Procedure
When I finish any project I throw the cut offs in a bin. I've accumulated quite a collection of scraps (see photo 1). What to do with them was my next question. I decided to make a plate. You can use any assortment of woods you have available.

1   Use a backer board (any ¼ in material) to glue all the pieces to it and to assist in holding all the pieces together when it is mounted on the lathe.

2   With a compass draw a 12 in circle in the middle of the board (see photo 2). I decided to begin with a focal point (I don't usually) which is the eye shape in the center (see photo 3).

3   Begin planing pieces that look good together (see photos 3, 4). Next fit them together. To make curved cuts I used my spindle sander.

4   To make the cuts use a table saw. I've mounted a laser on the saw (see photo 4) to show me exactly where the blade is going to cut. I scribe the line, set the fence so the laser lines up with the mark, and clamp it down and make the cut.

5   In the following photos I'll describe some of the steps I use to find all the angles that are needed in these types of projects. Photo 5 shows where the triangle piece is to be fitted. In photo 6 I've moved the two smaller pieces on the left out of the way for now, and slid the piece to be fitted up to the piece on the right. Place a straightedge against the piece of wood that has the angle that is needed, cut on this line, and check the fit. If the cut is off a little, adjust the fence and try again (see photo 7). I was close on my first try so I left the fence at whatever angle it was and just nibbled at the piece until it fit (see photo 8).

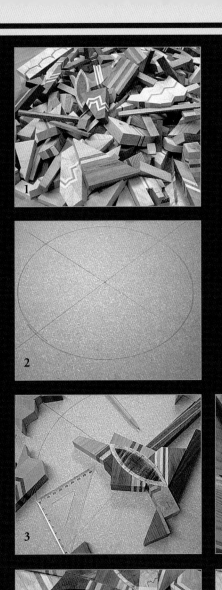

6   Slide another piece in place where the cut is going to be made to fit the piece. Using your straightedge scribe the cut to be made and mark it at this point (see photos 9 and 10). Cut on this mark and test fit.

7   If the fit isn't good, reset the fence and trim until the fit is satisfying (photos 11 and 12). Use a piece to scribe the angle needed to complete the piece by butting it up to the first piece and overlapping the piece to be scribed and cut.

8   Photo 13 shows all the pieces glued in place. Smooth the plate with a belt sander or a hand-held planer. I prefer to turn it smooth on the lathe.

9   Draw a 12 in circle and cut out on band saw. Mount the faceplate using screws long enough to go through the backer board only (see photos 14 and 15).

10   In photo 16 the plate is mounted and a recess is turned for the 4-way jaws. Remove and polish. When the polish is dry remove and mount the plate in the jaws and turn the shape.

Note   To cut small pieces that have the grain running in every direction use good quality cross cut carbide blade and a few hold-down clamps.

94

9

10

11

12

13

14

16

15

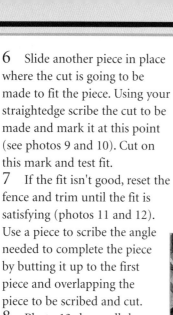

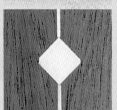

Index

A
alabaster trim bowl, 43
applewood candlestick, 59
aspen bowl, 21
B
balancing logs, 19
Bergen, Henry, 16
Bergen, Tim, 61
burls, 20
C
candleholders, 22
candlesticks, 91
centerwork, 6
chisels, 6, 11
chucks, 11
Colorwood, 9, 28, 29
Colorwood salt & pepper, 42
cut off sled jig, 74
cut out work, 14
cutting tools, 6
D
da Vinci, Leonardo, 4
drawings, 11
dust hazards, 7
dust marks, 7
Dymondwood, 9
Dymondwood pen & pencil, 43
Dymondwood salt & pepper, 42
E
electrostatic filters, 7
F
faceplate turning, 6
filters, 7
finishing, 15
      Danish oil, 15
      linseed oil, 15
      oil-based varnish, 15
      peanut oil, 15
      Pentacryl, 15
      teak oil, 15
      Turner's polish, 15
      Varathane, 15
      walnut oil, 15
food-safe finish, 15
G
gavel & stand, 45

getting started, 6
glue, 11
grinding, 11
gouges, 6, 11
H
Hazue, Harm, 44
Hiebert, John, 24
I
incorporating bark & fungus, 18
index, 96
introduction, 4
J
joinery, 14
K
kaleidoscope plate, 93
keepsake box & lid, 56
keepsake box pattern, 56
L
laminating, 14, 26, 28, 29, 30, 31, 32,
33, 41, 42, 45, 46, 49, 50, 53, 54, 56, 57,
59, 66, 67, 74, 75, 76, 77, 78, 79, 85, 86,
87, 88
laminating hints, 4, 11, 90
lathe set up, 11
leaf making, 91
lighthouse salt & pepper, 41
long chisel, 17
M
magnetic chess set, 39
making a box & lid, 12
making a vase & lid, 13
man-made wood, 9, 43
maple bowl, 22
maple leaf bowl, 84
maple vase, 18
measuring, 11, 12
N
newspaper wrap, 19
Norfolk pine box & lid, 12
Norfolk pine vase & lid, 13
O
oak & cherry bowl, 66
oak & cherry goblet, 70
P
Parallam wood, 9
parting tools, 6, 11

patterned vase, 49
patterned vase & handle pattern, 52
pen & pencil jig, 64
pen & pencil sets, 43-62
Pentacryl, 10, 15
perfume applicator, 43
pink rolling pin, 25
plain woodturning, 14
R
resins, 9, 43
Russian olive bowl, 21
S
safety 6
scroll work plate, 47
scroll work rim pattern, 48
sanding, 15
scraping, 6
segmentation, 14
segmented walnut bowl, 73
sharpening, 12
spalting 6
spindle turning, 6, 11
stabilizing fibers, 19
stabilizing steel cone, 17
stabilizing yoke, 17
striped rolling pin, 25
T
thunderbird bowl, 32
thunderbird cutting board, 31
thunderbird rolling pin, 27
tool rests, 6, 11
tool sharpening, 12
turning bowls, 20, 21
turning man-made materials, 9, 43
turning techniques, 14
turning vases, 13, 17, 18, 19
W
walnut bowl, 53
walnut bowl pattern, 55
wine cooler stand, 34
winged chess bowl, 38
wood collection, 6
wood grain, 10, 20
wood seasoning, 10
wood selection, 8
wood toxins, 7
work area, 7

References
Leier, Ray, etal, *Contemporary Turned Wood*, Hand Books Press, 1999.
Raffin, Richard, *Turning Wood*, The Taunton Press, 1985.
Rowley, Keith, *Woodturning*, Guild of Master Craftsman Publications Ltd., 1990.
    Woodturning magazine, Guild of Master Craftsman Publications Ltd., 2003, 2004, 2004, 2004.
    The Woodturners magazine, Highbury Nexus Special Interests Ltd., 2001, 2003.